D0909811

Pavlova

Photo. D'Ora

PORTRAIT STUDY OF PAVLOVA

THE GENIUS OF DANCE

Pavlova

BY WALFORD HYDEN

Her Former Musical Director

WITH ILLUSTRATIONS

Little, Brown, and Company

BOSTON   1931

Foreword

I HAVE been associated with Madame Anna Pavlova since 1910, when I conducted the performance of "La Fille Mal Gardée" at the Palace Theatre in London. As rehearsal pianist and often Musical Director, I have accompanied her on several English, Continental, and world tours; with the exception of the War period, when I was in the army, I have been constantly in touch with her for more than twenty years.

I mention these facts that the reader may understand I have some claim to try to present a personal and intimate picture of one who was loved and admired throughout the world. This book is not an attempt at a formal biography. It is a book of impressions and recollections set down while they are still warm in my memory.

My thanks are due to those who have assisted me in its preparation, and especially to M. Victor Dandré, her devoted husband, for his kind interest in it and his valuable help in the matter of illustrations.

London, 1931.   WALFORD HYDEN

Contents

Illustrations

Pavlova

CHAPTER I

The Genius

ANNA PAVLOVA was not merely a dancer. She was a genius of the dance. To her, dancing was even more than an art — it was a religion. She danced, in her brief intense life, before more people than any dancer who has ever lived; and she danced not merely for their amusement. To have seen Pavlova dance is to have had a spiritual experience, to have been in the presence of a Mystery — so great was her emotional power.

If what she has given to humanity cannot be compared in permanence with the gifts of others whom we designate as geniuses, it is not because Pavlova gave less than they in either quality or quantity; it is because the medium which she chose for the expression of her inspiration is a transitory medium. When the dancer dies, the dance is finished. It is therefore no easy matter to convey, particularly to the reader of the future who will

(3)

Pavlova

not have seen Pavlova, the fact from which there
is no escape for those of this generation who knew
her; that this woman was more than a dancer;
she was the embodiment of the Spirit of Dance.

In her profession she was as technically perfect
as it is possible for a human being to become. From
early childhood she had been trained in the most
severe of all schools of dancing — the Imperial
School of Ballet at the Czar's Court in St. Petersburg. But training alone does not explain the
triumphs of her world career. It was something
more than technique which caused her to be acclaimed everywhere as the greatest dancer.

She had that quality, peculiar to genius, of dealing with difficulties and obstacles as though they
did not even exist. When we consider that, despite
the jealousies and intrigues of the Imperial School
of Ballet, she had attained the highest grade, that
of *ballerina,* at the early age of twenty-two years;
when we consider that her success outside Russia
and throughout all the countries of the world for
more than twenty years afterwards was not merely
success but a triumphant progress; when we consider that Pavlova never failed, not even once,
anywhere, to arouse her audiences to enthusiasm,

we are confronted with the fact that her life is an example of the kind of success which comes so easily that it seems as though no difficulties or obstacles had barred the way.

Yet achievement of this kind is never a matter of luck. Her immediate triumph and her prolonged reign as the supreme dancer were due to a degree of emotional concentration which is that of inspiration alone.

Her life was spiritually organized with the fanaticism of an ascetic. She was devoted to dancing in every particle of her being; mentally and physically, she was organized for an intense rhythmic expression. It is in this respect that she was a religious phenomenon. She presents all the characteristics of single-minded devotion to an ideal — a devotion which resulted in the achievement of that ideal and the brushing aside of what would be insuperable obstacles for a person less concentrated in soul.

Dancing is a form of Magic. In its origin, it goes back to the ceremonial observances of the most primitive peoples. In the religious rites of antiquity — the Bacchanals and Eleusinian Mysteries of Greece — dancing was used as a means of invoking the gods; or, as rationalists would say, the forces of Nature, the unseen rhythmical powers of the universe — which, itself, never stops dancing. Even King David danced before the Lord, as the dervishes still dance, working themselves into a state of ecstasy. From the corroborees of the Australian blacks, from the war dances of the South Sea Islanders, from the Snake dances of the American Indians, from all these, and so many more manifestations of the ancient necessity to dance, is a great cultural but not a great emotional distance to the Imperial Russian Ballet. And just as the dance among primitive peoples has the effect of exhilarating the religious fervour of the tribes, so by her magic Anna Pavlova, moving widdershins and deosil, cast her spell over the civilized world.

She lived for the dance. Unless this be understood there is no possibility of understanding her. Everything that happened, every incident and experience in her career bore some relation to her art or was an expression of it. She was a dancer in her fibres, and it was with the movements of her body that she made her magical invocations.

I say *of her body,* advisedly; for dancing is

(6)

Pavlova

unique among the arts. A painter, a sculptor, a writer, a musician — even an actor — all make, to some extent, an "intellectual" contribution to humanity's pleasure and enlightenment. But dancing is the oldest of the arts and of them all is most directly an expression of emotions and instincts without intellectual overtones. It is wrong to "intellectualise" the character of a dancer. A dancer's intellect is of a peculiar kind. A dancer is body. A dancer is abstract ryhthm in the flesh. A dancer is music that is *watched*.

It is even a mistake to speak of Beethoven's ideas. One should speak of Beethoven's symphonies. How much more difficult is it to speak of Pavlova's "ideas!" She was not a theoretical thinker. She philosophized with her feet; and with every line and curve of her body, she showed beauty to the world in a practical, physical demonstration.

Of all the arts, dancing is the most direct plastic expression of the artist's emotions. The secret of Pavlova's achievement is that she was emotionally organized, mystically organized, for this physical rhythmic expression.

She was like a dynamo. She was always giving out energy and renewing it from within. Though

she looked frail, she was not frail. She was slight
of build, but enormously strong in her muscles.
Yet what she did was too much even for such a
finely muscled athlete to accomplish without the
driving power of a supernormal nervous force.
Day after day, week after week, month after
month, with only brief vacations, she gave nine or
ten performances a week, with the accompanying
ordeals of rehearsals, for more than twenty years.
Travelling everywhere without any relaxation,
sometimes even without proper sleep, she kept on
and on, doing a greater amount of actual physical
work than could have been expected from the most
robust of women. And when it is considered that
her work was full of moments more intense than
the average woman can ever hope to experience,
even once, in a lifetime, we realize that Pavlova was
a phenomenon and that her power was the inex-
haustible power of genius, nothing less.

How can I convey the impression of this vivid
electric creature, vibrating with energy, never still,
driving herself and all associated with her inces-
santly onwards from one town to another, from
one theatre to another, to performance after performance, all over the world, never pausing for

adequate rest, using herself up perpetually? Any one who has seen her in "Les Papillons" will understand what I mean. This dance lasts only forty seconds. Pavlova enters, quivering in every nerve, poised on the points of her toes, dancing, it would seem, with her fingertips and her eyelashes, to represent the flight of a butterfly. In the forty seconds of "Les Papillons", she could transform an audience, and one felt that the whole theatre was fluttering with butterflies like a garden in June. Such was the concentrated power of her art. It was the same in her life. She was like a butterfly — the creature of a brief summer who could never stop fluttering until she fell dead.

She worked so hard, she devoted herself so single-mindedly to her work, that all her energies were absorbed in it. When she danced, that was Pavlova. She lived her emotional life on the stage. Off the stage she was merely a dancer resting, recuperating for another public emotional outburst in the dance.

There are no "startling" revelations to be made about the private life of Anna Pavlova. Everything that is remarkable in her private life is explained by the fact that she lived for the dance

Pavlova

and for the dance alone. So great was her achievement, she had no need to create an adventitious
notoriety for herself. From this point of view, her
biography can never be so "sensational" as those
of lesser dancers; or of "unconventional" creators
in the other arts. Yet she was a remarkable woman.

The worst that can be stated of her character
had better be said at once: she was "temperamental." She was prone to such nasty fits of temper
(to give it a plain name) that at times it was difficult or impossible to work with her at all. These
outbursts were veritable storms of the nerves. Being
an artist, a woman, and a Russian, it would have
been unnatural if she had never given way to such
crises. She was obstinate and easily became excited,
and she was disagreeably selfish at times. Of this,
I shall have more to say later. It is enough to indicate here an attitude of respect and admiration for
her work which the memory of her excitability
cannot efface. Considering the nervous strain under
which she lived and worked, it is only remarkable
that the occasions of her temperamental outbursts
were not more frequent. In doing homage to the
art and genius of Anna Pavlova, I have no desire
to gloss the defects of her private character.

Pavlova

If she could be nasty at times, she could also be wonderfully charming. She could be as quick in the impulse of tenderness towards others and as trustful as a child; and as capricious and as captivating in her manner as a child.

In her private life, as in her dancing, she belonged to a pre-War and decent world. All through the modern "revolution" in art and everything else, Anna Pavlova danced her theories of artistic decency and personal grace before audiences that not even jazz crazes and distorted vogues could pervert in their appreciation of her. It may be that we shall "never look upon her like again." The cynical and sophisticated may say that Pavlova was a "back number" after the War, because she refused to dance ugliness. But into the lives of hundreds of thousands of people of all nationalities and all social degrees, she has brought a vision of loveliness that will remain when the pranks of distorted acrobats and poseurs have been forgotten. Classical grace and charm can never become *demodé*.

She represented in her person the climax of an aristocratic restraint and delicacy in art with centuries of tradition behind it, coming unbroken from the court of Louis XIV through the rare culture of Old Russia. Perfection was her aim. As a ballerina of the Imperial Ballet, she had learned from childhood that nothing else mattered but perfection in the dance, that everything in her life must be sacrificed to this end. That is at once the secret of her success and an explanation of the fact that her private life was without the incidents of drama. She had no time for anything other than dancing.

Of her ballets and divertissements, I have written more fully in the latter part of this book. She was recognized as the world's greatest exponent of classical ballet. Her preference in music was for the old melodic composers, and she kept to her preference throughout all the post-war insanity and ugliness in music and all art. As for jazz and the jazz idea, she did not even bother to become indignant about it. She knew it would pass, as in fact it is passing already.

It has often been said that Pavlova, although the ballerina supreme, never did anything actually to advance the art of the ballet; that she introduced no new conceptions of technique; and that her influence on new schools of thought was *nil*. To the extent that this was so, the fault was not with

Pavlova, but with her public. She made numerous attempts to break away from the *genre* of ballet to which her admirers had become accustomed; but her followers would have none of it. They insisted on seeing her once more in the ballets which already they knew. It was always the old favourites they clamoured for; and much as Anna Pavlova desired to present new ideas, new music, new *décor,* she could not contend against this overwhelming sentiment of her public. She never carried out her desire to present a ballet to the music of Bach because she knew that her audiences would not associate her with Bach.

All over the world, the name of Pavlova is associated with "The Swan", her greatest individual triumph. Then come "Valse Caprice", her "Bacchanale", "Rondino", and the "Gavotte Pavlova." These fragments were the favourites of audiences everywhere. Gradually, as the public clamoured for more and more of her divertissements, her name became inseparably linked with them. Yet compared with her dancing and character portrayals in the ballet proper, these little pieces were no more than the dessert after a banquet.

Pavlova

She never went out of her way to dazzle her audiences with her brilliant technique. Others could do that. For Pavlova, technique was only a means to an end, the most perfect expression possible of the theme of the dance. Nevertheless, behind her apparently simple movements, there was a prodigious command of technique which had only been acquired by years of unbelievably hard discipline, self-denial, tenacity and compelling ambition. The use of her hands was perhaps the most remarkable of her accomplishments. She could convey any expression, tragic or comic, and the whole gamut of emotions by gestures of her arms and even of her finger tips. But she was unexcelled, too, in arabesque — that balanced pose in which one leg is raised and pointed backwards; and when she flitted about the stage in the *pas de bourré,* as, for example, in "Giselle" when she crossed the stage in a diagonal line, while holding her lilies in both hands, she was able to convey such an impression of lightness and speed that one had the feeling of witnessing a miracle — she seemed not to touch the stage at all.

Had she not been a great dancer, she would have been one of the world's greatest actresses. She played the part of "Giselle" with such realism that not only did she hold the audience spellbound — in the scene where she loses her reason — but she affected the girls in the corps-de-ballet to such an extent that some of them could not restrain themselves, and with tears running down their cheeks would completely break down.

Her versatility was amazing. She could change from the tragedy of "Giselle" or the poignant characterization of "Amarilla", to play a few minutes later the part of the skittish and mischievous daughter in "La Fille Mal Gardée", enrapturing the audience and the Ballet Company alike with her delicious pranks and coquettish ways. When one considers that she would be Greek in "Dionysius", Egyptian in "The Egyptian Mummy", a Hindu Goddess in "Krishna" and "Rada", the Spirit of Life in "Les Préludes", a Persian Princess in "The Three Palms", a classic ballet dancer in "Chopiniana", the magic bird in "Russian Folk Lore", a fairy doll in "The Fairy Doll", a debutante in "Invitation to the Waltz" — to name at random but a few of her many ballets — one realizes to what extent she had schooled herself in adaptability. No other dancer could hope to portray so many dramatic characters in one repertoire, actually living the parts as she did.

It would not be reasonable to compare the dancing of Anna Pavlova with that of other individual dancers still living. But there is a comparison which her generation has had to make, a comparison between her art and that of another very great dancer whose name stands for something definite in achievement — Isadora Duncan. Comparison is not easy, because the two women belonged to different worlds. Behind Pavlova was a tradition extending unbroken from the origins of the ballet in Europe. She had assimilated the best teachings of the Italian Renaissance School as developed at Milan; she had assimilated the essence of the French classical ballet coming directly from the court of Louis XIV to the Court of Peter the Great; and she had been taught in Russia, where dancing forms part of the life of the millions and was crystallized to perfection in the Czar's court; and beyond all this, Pavlova was herself a mystic of the dance, able to give her personal emotional forces an expression through and beyond the perfected technique of a tradition of centuries.

Isadora Duncan came from America, representing the aspirations of a new civilization towards æsthetic expression. She, too, had undergone a discipline of training, but it was self-imposed. She, too, had great histrionic and interpretative gifts, and she harmonized herself with the forces of Nature by means of the dance. She taught Pavlova something. Isadora Duncan was a romanticist of the Dance, and Pavlova a classical exponent who had reached that point of perfection where individual expression shines through the classical medium. Without making unnecessary comparisons between the genius of these two great women, there is one reflection with which we might leave this subject. It cannot be disputed that Anna Pavlova, having once seen Isadora Duncan perform, could forthwith have copied any one of her dances in all its technical intricacies, but no one would contend for a minute that Isadora Duncan could have imitated Pavlova.

If, because of what she has done, and what she could do, and what she was, I ascribe to her here the title of genius, often so question-begging, it is because the drama is undeniably art, and the *dramatis personæ* include creative individuals. When Henry Irving, in "The Bells", transformed

melodrama into tragedy, that was theatrical crea-
tiveness. In precisely the same way Pavlova showed
that she could take the most trivial of themes,
such as that of "The Fairy Doll," and raise it beyond pantomime to pathos. Unlike the other great
actresses of history, she never spoke a word when
on the stage. She had neither the arias of Wagner
nor the declamatory cadences of Shakespeare to
help the audience realize what she had to convey.
On the stage she was silent. She had to rely upon
gesture and pose alone. Yet in her dance-dramas
she held audiences enthralled like the greatest of
Shakespearian tragic heroines — a heroine of
Shakespeare, without words.

CHAPTER II

Imperial School

OF Anna Pavlova's early life in Russia I cannot give first-hand information, as my association with her did not begin until she came to England. Pavlova herself has told me many of the facts here set down. I have gleaned others from various Russian members of her Company, chatting to while away the tedium of our long journeys.

I can quote the authority of Monsieur Svetloff in his obituary article in *La Russie Illustré*, for the statement that she was born in St. Petersburg in the year 1885. This means that she was forty-six years of age at the time of her death. She may have been a few years older than this. According to devious calculations made by members of her Company, her age was placed at fifty-one years; but, for the usual reasons, Pavlova herself gave no enlightenment, and it is doubtful whether any one would have been impolitic enough to have asked her. In the Company, her birthday was celebrated on February 16th (which is February 3d, Russian old style). Her "Name Day" was on January 30th. It is said that she was born a seven-months' child. Her father died when she was two years old.

According to the legend, Anna Pavlova spent a great deal of her childhood in the country. Her first inspiration came in the open air, when she felt compelled to dance with the butterflies in the summertime. A boy came and caught one of the butterflies and crushed it. That was Pavlova's first contact with dramatic tragedy. She felt "as if some giant had reached up his hand and pulled down the sky." In this story, there is the theme for a ballet in commemoration of her, should it ever come to be written.

The legend continues that as a little girl her mother took her to the Mariansky Theatre to see Tschaikowski's great ballet in four acts, "The Sleeping Beauty." As they reached the theatre, her mother said, "Now, my little Nura, you will enter fairyland." Pavlova has described on various occasions how she sat numbed, with her fingers clenched until the nails brought blood from her palms, and how she almost swooned for joy, so intense was the experience. That night she could not sleep, and the next day she began dancing and dancing what she could remember of the ballet. She persistently told her mother that one day she would dance the principal part in that ballet. The impulse did not pass like most inspirations of childhood. She persisted until, two years later, on her tenth birthday, her mother entered her as a pupil in the Imperial School of Ballet attached to the Mariansky Theatre. The time came when she danced indeed the rôle of "The Sleeping Beauty" — and so many others besides; and the point of this story is that she adapted Tschaikowski's ballet to her own purposes, giving it the name of "Visions."

From the day that Anna Pavlova entered the Imperial School of Ballet, she was consecrated to her career. It is unlikely that the conditions which created the discipline and curriculum of that school will ever recur. The pupils were trained like neophytes in a religion. Dancers they had to become.

Peter the Great established formal ballet dancing in Russia. It is said that he, himself, took part in the ballets and that his dancing was good. He had taken the idea of a court ballet from France where, on the lawns of the "Sun King" at Versailles, classical dancing under Italian tuition was a feature of the court life. In Russia, the Imperial Ballet continued to be instructed by French dancing masters, including the famous Didlot, and to enjoy the personal patronage of the sovereign. The daughter of Peter the Great, the Empress Elizabeth, made even more elaborate provision for the school than her sire had done.

Owing to the isolation of Russia, it was the Russian Imperial School of Ballet, alone in Europe, which, after the bourgeois revolutions in the West, carried on the grand manner in dancing. But owing to the peculiar Russian national gift for dancing as a mystic expression, that tradition came in time to be distinctive in itself. It was the combination of a classical form with a romantic expression which so astounded Western Europe when Diaghiliev took the Russian ballet westwards.

With a discipline more rigid than that of any military academy, the children who entered the School of Ballet were trained physically until their

supple young limbs were muscled for feats of
dancing which no adult could have acquired with
any amount of training. Also they were given a
general education. Children could not be admitted to the school without a strict preliminary
scrutiny of their soundness of physique and natural
gift for dancing.

The following account of the school is that given
by Mr. Rothay Reynolds (quoted by J. E. Crawford Flitch, *Modern Dancing and Dancers* —
Richards, 1912):

The school contains a great room for dancing, with
a floor sloped at the same angle as that of the stage at
the Mariansky Theatre. Here one may see a class of
merry boys instructed in their art. A master, usually
one of the best dancers in the theatre, shows them the
steps and movements to be learnt, and half-a-dozen do
their best to copy him. After ten minutes they go and
rest, and a second batch comes forward. The boys seem
to enjoy the work, and even when they are supposed
to be resting some of them will continue to practise and
give each other friendly hints. In another and similar
room is the girls' class, where the method is the same.
Then there is a room with many toilet-tables on which
grease-paints are set out, and with mirrors and electric

lights arranged exactly as at the theatre. Here the pupils assemble for lessons in make-up. A boy has to learn to transform himself into a Chinese or an old man or a beautiful young Greek, and he has to pass examinations at different points of his school career in this art. I remember once meeting a young man in the waiting room of a Polish dentist (he goes on to relate). He told me he had toothache and a nervous break-down, brought on he believed by the strain of a difficult examination. I asked what were the subjects of the examination. "French", he said, "because we must be cultured, dancing, the history of dancing and painting my face." I had the curiosity to ask where this unusual curriculum was followed. "At the Imperial School of Ballet," he said, mentioned his name with the air of one who felt that he ought to have been recognized, and added: "Thank heaven I've passed, and now I am a premier danseur. It is a delightful life, and when I am too old to dance the State will give me a pension."

Anna Pavlova made rapid progress at the school. According to Monsieur Svetloff, who was present at her final examination when she danced the part of a dryad in a complicated little ballet of the school pupils, "She attracted the attention of every one with her thin, almost childish figure, and her dreamy face. In her poise and her manner of dancing, one felt that something great and classical had appeared. In her miming, there was nothing forced and studied — it was purely spontaneous."

M. Svetloff informs us that her early parts in ballet proper were Frost in "The Seasons of the Year", Zulmé in "Giselle", Aurore in "The Awakening of Flora", The Fairy Candide in "The Sleeping Beauty", and Fleur de Lys in "Esmeralda." Later she danced Lisa in "The Magic Flute", Juanita in "Don Quixote", Pierrette in "Arlequinade", and the Chief Naiad in "Sylvia." At last she got the title rôle of "Giselle", thus realizing her highest ambition.

Among her instructors was Gerdt and the illustrious Petipa himself. The *ballerine assolute* at the time were Mmes. Kschesinskaya, Legnani, and later, Preobrajenskaya. In addition to the inspiration of such brilliant seniors, Pavlova went during vacation time to Milan where she studied dancing under the greatest teacher of them all, Cecchetti. In later years, when she visited Milan with her own Company, I always noted that Anna Pavlova danced at her very best there. This was because Cecchetti was in a box watching her. She loved him like a father. He would come back of the stage after the performance and criticize her work chidingly or approvingly, as though she were the little girl he knew years before. Before Cecchetti she was humble, always. The discipline of the Imperial School of Ballet militated against presumptuousness on the part of the pupils toward their instructors.

Pavlova has often told me of her happy days at the Imperial School and the Mariansky Theatre. Her eyes would light up with enthusiasm as she spoke of the virtuosity of the great ballerinas who reigned there when she was a beginner. According to her account, the ballet was a distinctly exclusive institution in aristocratic Russia. All the seats and boxes in the theatre were booked perpetually by devotees of the ballet, known as *balletomanes,* who never missed a performance. She told me that when one of these old gentlemen died there would be as many as a hundred applications for the vacant seat. The *balletomanes* were keen protagonists of the various ballerinas, and would angrily dispute their respective merits in the foyer of the theatre during the intervals in the performance. When one of the great ballerinas travelled to Moscow, she would be followed there by her devoted admirers.

Pavlova

A curious incident occurred when Pavlova was a very small girl at the Imperial School. The Czar, in accordance with his annual custom, paid a ceremonial visit to the school, and the children performed for him a little ballet designed for the occasion. The Czar was so pleased with the dancing of the children that he picked up one of the little girls in his arms (not Pavlova) and kissed her. Every one was delighted at this so human action from one so exalted, who was regarded with almost superstitious fear and reverence as the Little Holy Father of all the Russians — everybody, that is, except Nura Pavlova. She wept bitterly because the Czar had not kissed her; whereupon the Little Father, understanding the child's disappointment, kissed Pavlova also! I mention this little story because it shows that, from her earliest days, Pavlova was accustomed to getting what she wanted by one means or another, without stopping to count the cost.

When she was an advanced pupil at the school, the famous Italian ballerina, Legnani, visited St. Petersburg and danced at the Mariansky Theatre. She was a fine muscular woman and she absolutely astonished the Russians in particular because she could perform the feat of doing thirty-two *fouettés* in succession. The Russian dancers were humiliated because of their own comparative incapacity. But Pavlova went away quietly and practised this extraordinarily difficult movement until at last after some weeks, she, too, was able to do thirty-two *fouettés*. One day, in the practise room, she proudly asked everybody present to watch her doing an imitation of Legnani. She thereupon proceeded to do her thirty-two *fouettés* to the consternation of all present.

The ballet master, Gerdt, went up to her, furious. Instead of the praise she had expected, he almost shook her in his rage. "Leave acrobatics to others, Anna Pavlova!" he shouted. "It is positively more than I can bear to see the pressure such steps put upon your delicate muscles and the arch of your foot." Pavlova hung her head, ashamed. She said, "I, too, want to become a great dancer and to be praised like Legnani for doing thirty-two *fouettés*. I am not strong like the others here and I only wanted to show you that I can do anything at all with practice." Gerdt said to her, with a strange softness in his voice, "Now you have shown us that you can do the most difficult acro-

Photo. Edw. S. Curtis Studios, Los Angeles

PAVLOVA IN A CHARACTERISTIC POSE

batic feats, I beg you never to try again to imitate those who are stronger than you in their muscles. You must realize that your daintiness and fragility are your greatest assets. You should always do the kind of dancing which brings out your own rare qualities instead of trying to win praise by mere acrobatic tricks."

A curious fact which ought to be put on record is that during the political upheavals of the year 1905, when all Russia was in a ferment owing to the shooting of the student demonstrators and the priest Gapon, Pavlova and Fokine took part in organizing a strike among members of the Imperial Ballet. There were meetings at Fokine's flat and also at Pavlova's flat, at which resolutions were passed demanding higher rates of pay and better conditions of work. Pavlova was most scornful of other members of the Ballet who were timid at these meetings, or who wished to get the advantages of the agitation without running any of the risks. She told me that she and Fokine made impassioned speeches appealing for solidarity and so on, in the best trade-union manner; and that after the disturbances had quieted down, an attempt was made to have her removed from the Ballet because of the part she had played in this agitation. However, the government officials and everybody else concerned were only too glad to forget all that had happened during that brief upheaval, and no retributory action was taken against her.

In the year 1907, Isadora Duncan visited Russia. She created at first great amusement by her theories of dancing nude. She was told among other things that Russia in the depth of winter was hardly a place for advocating returns to nature; but that if she felt inclined to give a demonstration, no doubt the public would be highly entertained if she would give an exhibition of barefoot dancing on the Neva with the temperature at sixty degrees below zero.

But after the first laughter had died down, people began to take a little more notice of Duncan. Fokine, in particular, was deeply impressed by her opinions that the music of Chopin and Schumann was more suitable for dancing than the conventional ballet music of Minkus and Drigo. He said in despair to Petipa, "Oh, if we only had a dancer with the sensibility of Isadora Duncan and the technique of Kschesinskaya!" Petipa was then already an old man, a Marseillais, who had been in

Russia since the 1860's — and had never yet learned to speak Russian properly. He was naturally not particularly impressed with "Duncanism", but he said with a dry emphasis in his broken accent: "There is one of our dancers who has all the feeling of Duncan and all the technique of Kschesinskaya. You know whom I mean — Anna Pavlova."

It is difficult to say exactly to what extent Isadora Duncan was the inspiration of the new style in Russian ballet which caused Diaghiliev and his Company to "break away" and begin their long series of experiments in modernism which culminated in such works as "Les Noces" and "Pas d'Acier", but it is certain that the famous American dancer brought to Russia a stimulus which enabled the discontent of Fokine and others to culminate in action. While Duncan was still in Russia, Fokine arranged and produced a *pas de trois* entitled "Eunice", danced by himself with Pavlova and Tamara Karsavina, which was definitely in the new style.

By this time, Pavlova had become a ballerina. She had passed in quick succession through the lower grades and already she was set down to succeed Preobrajenskaya on the latter's retirement from the position of *ballerina assoluta*. This last formal promotion never came. Pavlova left the Czar's ballet and set out to show the whole world what she could do.

During the vacation at the Mariansky Theatre in April, 1908, Pavlova made the first of that long series of tours which never ended until her death. Taking with her a company of twelve girls and eight men, she went to Helsingfors in Finland, the company being under the management of M. Fazer. She then left Russia for the first time and went to Stockholm, Copenhagen, Prague, Vienna and Berlin, thence returning to St. Petersburg.

At Stockholm, the enthusiastic crowd surrounded her hotel, clamouring for her after the performance until long after midnight. Pavlova could not understand that she had become a "star" and that the applause was for her personally, instead of for the whole Ballet. From the balcony window of her hotel, she threw the flowers from her bouquets amongst the crowd in an attempt to appease what looked very much like a riot! Her maid had to tell her that the people were there to applaud her because she had brought joy into their

Pavlova

lives. It is said that not until this moment did Pavlova fully realize that she was ready to achieve her world purpose.

As for the impression which already she had made upon the Russian audiences at the Mariansky Theatre, I conclude this chapter with some notes specially and very kindly written for inclusion in this book by Prince Georg Kotschubey, one of the very first patrons of the Russian Ballet to realize the genius of Pavlova, and one who remained her devoted friend and admirer until the end. It is with deep gratitude that I acknowledge Prince Kotschubey's kindness in allowing me to reproduce here extracts from a letter to me in which he describes those brilliant days:

"My family always had a box at the Imperial Theatre, and from my earliest days," (he writes), "I used to visit the brilliant performances of opera and ballet which were given there. I first began to take serious notice of the ballet as a form of art when I was a student at the Emperor Alexander College in 1899.

"The Russian Imperial Ballet at this time was giving performances which were unique in the world. They were lavishly subsidised by the Imperial Exchequer. To give an idea of the way in which things were done, at a performance of a new ballet entitled "The Corsair" there were real sailing boats brought on to the stage, shown at sea during a terrific storm. A whole battalion of one of the crack regiments of Guards, the soldiers of which were noted for the fact that they were the tallest in the Russian Army, were placed at the disposal of the stage manager (Aistoff) who trained them for some weeks as follows: They first lay down in ranks at full length on the enormous stage, covered by a huge stage cloth, painted to represent the sea. Then, at indicated moments, they pushed the cloth upwards with their hands, giving an extraordinarily realistic effect of the ocean's undulations. As the tempest increased, the concealed guardsmen rose rhythmically to their knees, and eventually to their full height, creating an astonishing illusion of a tempest with great waves sweeping over the stage. The cost of the production of this ballet was 500,000 gold roubles.

"The orchestra at the Mariansky Theatre consisted of 120 instrumentalists under the direction of Drigo. The leader of the orchestra was Leopold Auer, and the harpist was Zabel. The *corps-de-ballet* itself consisted of several hundred dancers, and it was an unforgettable spectacle when, during an ensemble, with this enormous number of dancing figures on the stage, one of the *ballerine* would dance a brilliant pizzicato or a difficult variation with *fouettés* taken at a lightning speed.

"At the beginning of the century, the Mariansky ballet was dominated by Kschesinskaya and Legnani in clas-

sical dancing. The principal male dancers were Marius
Petipa, Stoukolkin, Bekeffi. These were the stars who succeeded Zucci, Jure, Grimaldi and Roslarlevoy; the last
having died tragically young.

"It follows that little Anna Pavlova, then a young
dancer in the ranks of the ballet, had small opportunity
of shining out an individual.

"At that time the crown of supremacy was being disputed between Kschesinskaya and Legnani. The beautiful *premiers sujets* who were quite soon to reach the
position of *ballerine* were Preobrajenskaya, Trefilova,
and Sedova, amongst others, who only occasionally appeared in the principal rôles in short ballets, and even
with their brilliant talents were mostly known as dancers in support of Kschesinskaya or Legnani; who, between them, took the principal parts in the big ballets
which were performed. It was impossible for the most
critical expert in ballet to award the palm either to
Kschesinskaya, whose gentle and dainty talent was
shown in such ballets as "Esmeralda", "Paquita", and
"The Pharaoh's Daughter", or to the abnormal technical gifts of Legnani, when she did her gossamer thirty-
two *fouettés* in "Le Cheval Bossu" to the accompaniment
of thunderous applause from the whole enthusiastic
audience.

"So secure were Legnani and Kschesinskaya in their
own artistry and in the public favour, that they could
afford to be indifferent to the advancement of any of

the young Russian Ballet artists. But it was a very different matter for those of lesser rank who had been already advanced in the preliminary promotions from the rank and file of the *corps-de-ballet*. After eight years of strict training at the Imperial School, the whole corps seemed to be composed of picked dancers. Every dancer who appeared at that Theatre was of graceful physique and beautiful to behold; and all had secret hopes and ambitions in their hearts. When it was a question of deciding promotion, it was absolutely impossible for the Ballet Master to say that one should be preferred more than another. It was only by intuition that the authorities could guess that this dancer or that was likely to become artistically supreme in the future.

"It was when I was eighteen years old that I, with three other young 'men about town' who loved the Ballet (friends who have now passed away — Platon Zachrevsky, Joseph Schatilov, André Raevsky) managed after great difficulty to obtain permanently, for all ballet performances, possession of a luxurious box, No. 26, on the *belle-étage*. How proud we were! Directly below us was the box of Kschesinskaya. Directly opposite us was the box of Emperor Nicholas II. In line with us, in the front rows of the stalls, sat the Ministers of State and members of the aristocracy who held their seats hereditarily.

"It was in such surroundings that I first saw Anna Pavlova. She was in the very back row among hundreds of brilliant dancers, but her fragile spiritual personality attracted attention at once and hypnotized our young hearts. There was something superhuman in this Sylphide.

"It was impossible at first for us to discover her name, because entrance to the stage at the Mariansky Theatre was forbidden to everybody except members of the Imperial Family. At this time nobody knew the name of her who was to become our national pride and genius. Yet I believe that not only we young bloods, but many others also in the theatre, understood that a great genius was in this young girl.

"It was Kschesinskaya who, at the gala performance in honour of her ten years at the Mariansky Theatre, used her influence to advance Pavlova. Owing to the exceptional service which Kschesinskaya had rendered to the Theatre she was given a benefit performance after only ten years, instead of the usual twenty years. Never have I seen a more impressive gala performance on any stage in the world. When the curtain rose after the second act, in the presence of the whole Imperial Family, the Ministers of State, and the Foreign Ambassadors, the stage was like a gorgeous conservatory. Baskets of flowers twice as high as Kschesinskaya were there in abundance. For more than half an hour attendants continually brought her the most beautiful presents.

"It was at this performance that our dear Anna Pavlova was first advanced to the front of the stage. Only then did her career as an individual artist begin. A divine ray of happiness was shining on her thin young face.

"The very next day, after the completion of my studies, having discovered her address, I called, with my heart beating furiously, at her home in one of the small streets in St. Petersburg — Kolomenskaya. After passing through the second court of an apartment house and walking up dilapidated steps, I nervously pressed the bell of her flat. The door was opened to me by the mother of Anna Pavlova. I was kindly invited into the small sitting room. In a few seconds there came fluttering in the one for whom I had been waiting with a beating heart. There, slim as a flower-stem, dark, with clever thoughtful eyes, before me stood Anna Pavlova who in days to come was to conquer the world.

"Amazingly simple, full of exuberance and vitality, and exceptionally feminine, there was yet a wonderful gentleness in her movements and in her way of speaking. We began to speak about art, both in the spirit of youthful ardour. For hours on end she spoke of her art with love and fanaticism. In her eyes was the light of a strong will and a deep belief in herself. Speaking very excitedly she declared that she would become world famous or else disappear utterly from the horizon. No half measures for her! This deep belief in God's will and in herself created a profound impression upon me which will never disappear from my memory. I knew at once that this slender being would make every possible sacrifice for her art, and that she would attain her purpose, and that nothing but a miracle of Fate could prevent her.

"We parted as good friends, and after that I frequently visited the little flat in Kolomenskaya. I introduced all my friends to her, and we did our best to give pleasure to "little Nura" by arranging Zigeuner parties, troika excursions, and so on.

"Ever since then, I have watched her career. Despite her genius and the recognition of it by the Russian public, Anna Pavlova could not at once reach the supreme rank in the dancing hierarchy of the Mariansky Theatre. She broke the Gordian knot by leaving the Mariansky Theatre and accepting an engagement as prima ballerina in Diaghiliev's International Ballet.

"In accepting Diaghiliev's offer she was at first diffident, but when she was approached a second time by Diaghiliev she took fate by the forelock. It should be realized that any artist who had for twenty years been dancing on the Imperial stage was entitled to retire on a State pension. To leave the Mariansky Theatre in such circumstances was considered to be tantamount to madness, as resignation involved forfeiture of the pension. Yet Anna Pavlova made the decision against all the claims of tradition and expediency. Her intuition was right.

"Her invitation performances in Diaghiliev's Ballet in Paris in the spring of 1909 attracted European notice.

Pavlova

Thereafter, when she returned to her own Mariansky Theatre by special invitation, she was impatiently waited for and loved by the whole Russian people. "Giselle" was her crowning achievement, the greatest expression of her genius in choreographic art.

"The expression of her face was unforgettable — sensitive, nervous, and utterly unlike that of any other human being. The finest painters and sculptors have endeavoured to represent her features on canvas and in stone — but without success, so far as I know, except for the two Russian painters, Seroff and Sorin. I remember on one of her last visits to Hamburg, Professor Lederer, the well-known German sculptor, a great admirer of Pavlova, came specially to make studies of her features. After several sittings he complained to me that after a hundred different attempts to sketch her remarkable face, he had to abandon the hope of beginning a big work, because every impression he obtained was different, as her very features changed with the fleeting of her moods."

CHAPTER III

World Fame

SHE needed worlds to conquer. Pavlova could
never have remained satisfied even with the rapt
admiration of the St. Petersburg *balletomanes*.
Having become a ballerina, there was every induce-
ment for her to remain in the Imperial Ballet.
There she was able to choose the ballets in which
she wished to appear and to dance when she wanted
to dance and not otherwise. She need only have
given six performances a month, and, at the age
of thirty-five, glorious, she could have retired on a
State pension.

Therefore, she left the Imperial Ballet. She had
"attained" there. It had served its purpose.

Instead of dancing six times a month for the joy
of the Russian *balletomanes,* she elected to dance
eight or ten times a week for the joy of all the peoples of the world. Instead of retiring sedately on a

pension, she preferred to keep on dancing until she dropped dead from the exhaustion of it.

In April of the year 1909 Pavlova decided to make a second European tour. Accordingly, with a supporting company, she visited once more Stockholm, Copenhagen, Berlin and Vienna, for short seasons in each of these capitals. Everywhere her reception was memorable. On her second appearance in Stockholm, the enthusiastic crowd took the horses from her carriage and drew her themselves back to her hotel. The King of Sweden decorated her with a medal.

In May and June of 1909 she was in Paris, where she danced with the Diaghiliev Company.

Despite the fact that Pavlova had made European tours, it is of course to M. Diaghiliev that the whole credit must be given of having brought the Russian Ballet proper out of Russia into Western Europe. In Russia, he was esteemed as a wealthy patron of the ballet and one with a great knowledge of all the arts. He realized that the discontent which existed among the more ambitious and intelligent of the dancers was due to their desire to break away from the strict classical traditions of the Court theatre and to make experiments in choreography, *décor,* and music which would have been perhaps annoying to the older generation, schooled in the traditions of Petipa.

Therefore M. Diaghiliev represented to the Russian Government the great propaganda value for Russian Art which would ensue from his being allowed to take a company into Western Europe. He obtained permission and secured, in addition, the promise of a subsidy of fifty thousand rubles under one remarkable proviso — that a certain ballerina, who was a favourite of the official dealing with the transaction, should appear in the leading rôles.

When Pavlova arrived in Paris in May, 1909, Diaghiliev promptly offered her the principal rôles in four of his ballets: "Les Sylphides", "Spectre de la Rose" (with Nijinsky as partner), "Cleopatra" and "Pavillon d'Armide." The other ballerina, who brought with her talents the substantial subsidy in rubles, became jealous of Pavlova and refused to dance with her in any of Diaghiliev's productions. Diaghiliev was in a dilemma, but he refused to go back on his arrangement with Pavlova and lost the subsidy as a result.

The reception of the Diaghiliev Ballet in Paris

at the Châtelet Theatre is a matter of history. The Parisians were quick to perceive that something monumentally new had appeared in the world of art. Apart from Pavlova, the dancers included Nijinsky, Karsavina, Trefilova, and many others of that brilliant Russian constellation of stars which has since come to represent the very highest achievement of the art of ballet as we understand it in the twentieth century. The choreography of Fokine, the *décor* and costumes of Bakst, the conducting of Tscherepnine, only added to the virtuosity in dancing and in mime of the whole astounding company.

People wondered what the Russian Ballet must be like in Russia, if a travelling company could show such work as this. But the fact is that the Russian Ballet in Russia was thrilling and spectacular in quite a different way from Diaghiliev's Russian Ballet in Paris and London. Diaghiliev was a radical in ballet. The Mariansky tradition was that against which he was in revolt. But, like every innovator, he established his work on that already existing. Europe was astounded perhaps as much by the fact of the Russian Ballet itself as by Diaghiliev's innovations.

Pavlova

Pavlova shared the success of the Diaghiliev Ballet in Paris, but with so much talent about her, she felt, no doubt, that she needed to conquer her new worlds by herself.

King Edward VII, hearing of her reputation in Paris, had her invited to England for a private performance. Accordingly she danced in 1909 before the King and Queen of England at a reception given by Lady Londesborough. Following this visit, she left Diaghiliev and accepted an engagement to dance with Mikhail Mordkin and a small Company as an act in the vaudeville programme at the Palace Theatre in May, 1910. It was Alfred Butt (now Sir Alfred) who engaged her. A story is told of the theatrical agent who was rude when she called on him. He had never heard of the Mariansky Theatre, still less of Anna Pavlova, the ballerina. He told her to call again and bring her tights and he would see what she could do!

Her reception by the public in London showed immediate recognition of the fact that something remarkable had "arrived." Her dancing was the talk of London. The leaders of London society vied with one another in claiming acquaintance with her, and happy indeed was the society hostess who could manage to persuade Anna Pavlova to appear at a reception. Books of poems to Pavlova were published. Anagrams on her name appeared in the Press. From that moment there was no doubt that a new world-figure in art had won recognition.

The dance which took London by storm was her "Bacchanale", danced with Mordkin. It was the first time that London audiences had ever seen anything of the kind, an authentic Bacchanale danced in a frenzy of abandon to the spirit of revelry and drunkenness. The music from Glazounow's "Seasons" had a quick 2/4 beat, incessant, unrelaxing, urging the dance onwards like a pulse of fury. At the conclusion of the dance, her partner would fling her away from him, and she would fall with a crash, which made one think that she must have injured herself. A cry of horror would come from the audience — "She's hurt!" But Pavlova would bounce up like a figure of India rubber (having taken the precaution to fall properly for her rebound). Mordkin was a wonderful figure of a man, like a Greek god in physique. Pavlova was at the very prime of her youthful energy and enthusiasm. To add to the excitement of Londoners, she quarrelled with Mordkin on one occasion dur-

PAVLOVA AND LAURENT NOVIKOFF IN "BACCHANALE"

ing the "Bacchanale" and publicly slapped his face. Thereafter she refused to dance with him. The scandal-loving London public could not resist going to the Palace Theatre night after night to see if the pair would appear together again — a superb pair — in this positive orgy of a dance.

She came to London just at the right time. She was lucky and she was wise. The art of ballet in England had reached its height in the early days of Queen Victoria when Taglione was supreme. The climax of this early Victorian period of ballet was the famous *pas de quatre* in 1845, in which Lucille Grahn, Fanny Cerito, Carlotta Grisi and Taglione danced before Queen Victoria — an event which created a European sensation, because on this occasion a veritable constellation of stars shone in one spot of the theatrical firmament.

After that, the ballet declined in England. It would not be correct to say that when Anna Pavlova appeared in London the ballet was absolutely dead in England. Far from it. At the Empire and the Alhambra there were schools of ballet; and it must never be forgotten that Adeline Genée was the darling of the English public as a classical danseuse pure and simple, long before the appearance of Pavlova. But the ballet in England during the first ten years of the century had become conventionalized, particularly with regard to gesture and miming. What astonished and delighted London was the emotional power of Anna Pavlova's interpretations, combined as it was with her classical perfection of technique.

Besides Genée, London had seen the dancing of Isadora Duncan as early as the year 1900 — and the "barefoot" school of dancing developed by — for example — Maud Allan.

But for the most part, dancing as art was in disrepute. The ballets at the Empire and the Alhambra were merely interspersed with a variety programme and only too much of the dancing was frigid and neat and apparently without any inspiration. The first Russian danseuse to be seen in London was Lydia Kyasht, but although she represented some of the achievements of the Imperial School of Ballet, her work was of a different kind from that of Pavlova. Lydia Kyasht was ranked in Russia as *premier sujet*.

It is not too much to say, however, that the dancing of Adeline Genée and Isadora Duncan and Lydia Kyasht prepared London audiences for the coming of Pavlova. These dancers had shown the English public that dancing is an art and not merely a vaudeville act. When Pavlova appeared she showed the possibilities of the dance as one of the highest forms of art. Her "Bacchanale" with Mordkin was a revelation. Had she come earlier, the public would not have understood her work so well. Had she come later, Diaghiliev and his company would have been the revelation. But the Diaghiliev Company did not come to London until June, 1911, a year after Pavlova.

She came exactly at the right time. The melodious name of Anna Pavlova came to stand for something essentially vital in the art of the dance. Like every genius in the history of mankind, she knew how to choose her hour.

After her first appearance, her triumph, at the Palace Theatre, the public naturally clamoured for "more." She began a second London season in 1910 with an extended company in support. For the first time in England she now danced in a ballet — "La Fille Mal Gardée"; and it is at this point that my association with her began. I acted as pianist at the rehearsals, and then one evening, at exceptionally short notice, I was called on to conduct the orchestra for the performance of "La Fille Mal Gardée."

Her appearance before the London public in this ballet only confirmed her great reputation. As the skittish and mischievous "daughter", Pavlova had every opportunity to display her effervescent gaiety and the liveliness of her comedy miming. The effect in contrast with the "Bacchanale" was one of cultivated daintiness and polish. She had the audiences in a continual state of merriment. In her Pizzicato solo, she was lightness itself, and in the 3/4 Adagio (danced with her partner Novikoff — Mordkin having departed to America) she conveyed the tenderness of sentiment and romance in a sustained movement which, after so many quick movements earlier in the ballet, came with charming restfulness.

Despite the fact that the audience was enraptured, Chiriaieff, the ballet-master, was thoroughly displeased with the first performance of "La Fille Mal Gardée." After the bouts of applause had at last died away, he ordered the tired company to begin *at once* on a rehearsal. Every one adjourned to Pavlova's home at Hampstead, Ivy House, and the rehearsal lasted all that night.

Pavlova

In addition to "La Fille Mal Gardée", Pavlova's repertoire included "The Swan." To the cool 'cello music of Saint-Saëns, with its flowing harp accompaniment like the sound of quiet waters, she seemed to float upon the surface of a stage lit with a blue and mystic light, until the audience felt the chill of gracious death, and would become silent, in that tremolo of awe which is the tribute paid only to the greatest of dramatic artists at their greatest moments. As the last note of the music died away and the Swan lay there stilled, a deep hush would come over the theatre which nobody would dare break with applause. For more than ten seconds the dancer would receive this, the greatest of possible tributes to her power, before the unleashed acclamations began.

No wonder that she was described as "the dancing revelation of the age!" At the Palace Theatre, I have seen so many floral tributes that the stage was entirely covered with them, in layers, and not a square inch of the boards was visible. Almost every one in the audience had sent flowers — from peers to humble working people.

She began a tour through England with her Company. I remember that at Liverpool the queue for the matinée extended completely around the theatre, and people who had waited since the early morning could not secure admission to her afternoon performance; yet they waited through the matinée in order not to miss her in the evening. Usually her dressing room was so encumbered with bouquets, the tributes of her admirers, that it was impossible to move in it and the flowers had to be taken outside and stacked in the corridors.

Sometimes it was difficult for Pavlova to leave the theatre after a performance on account of the crowds besieging the stage door, waiting to get a close glimpse of her. I have seen young mothers with babies in their arms, struggling to be in the front rank of the crowd surging between the stage door and her car. They would hold their babies to Pavlova as she passed, begging her to touch the little ones, as though in her person she had some mystic energy which she was able to transmit by the laying on of hands.

On this first tour, although she travelled with a large Company, it was thought that dancing alone could not provide a sufficient entertainment. Her performances, therefore, included vocal and instrumental numbers besides a dramatic sketch. The

Pavlova

English public at that time had not been educated
to the enjoyment of an evening devoted entirely to
ballet.

I have beside me, preserved amongst the odds
and ends of bygone days, a programme of Pavlova's
second English tour on which I was with her Company as pianist and sub-conductor — Theodore
Stier being musical director. For its historical interest I reproduce this programme here:

First Visit to Harrogate of
Mdlle.

ANNA PAVLOVA

The Dancing Revelation of the Age
(Under the direction of Mr. Daniel Mayer.)

Together with
Mons. Novikoff
and the
Members of the Imperial Russian Ballet
including
Mons. Chiriaieff, Mlle. Gashewska, and Mlle. Roshanara

PROGRAMME

1. Overture........"Ruy Blas"...... *Mendelssohn*
   THE MUNICIPAL ORCHESTRA

(53)

Pavlova

2. 'Cello Solos (a) "Andante" ....*Schumann*

                (b) "Rondo" ....*Dvorak*

            MR. PAULO GRUPPE

    At the Piano — MR. WALFORD HYDEN

3. Mazurka ....*Glinka*

MLLE. KUHN	M. NIKITIN
MLLE. FREDOWA	M. MONAHOFF
MLLE. ZALMANOWA	M. TIKHOMIROFF
MLLE. PLASKOWIECZKA	M. KURILOFF

4. Danse Espagnole ....*Rubinstein*

    MLLE. GASHEWSKA AND M. SHOUBALOFF

5. Coquetteries de Columbine..............*Drigo*

    (Arranged by LEGAT)

    ANNA PAVLOVA

    MM. NOVIKOFF AND CHIRIAIEFF

Interval

6. Intermezzo from "The Jewels of the Madonna".....................*Wolf-Ferrari*

    THE MUNICIPAL ORCHESTRA

7. Indian Dances...................................

Indian God Dance	Warrior Dance
Harvest Dance	Snake Dance

    MLLE. ROSHANARA

(54)

Pavlova

8. Arias (a) Santuzza Aria
   ("Cavalleria Rusticana")...*Mascagni*
   (b) "Dich theure Halle" ....*Wagner*
   (with Orchestra)

   MISS HELEN FAIRBANK

9. Extracts from the Grand Ballet "Coppelia"..*Delibes*
   Mazurka

MLLE. GASHEWSKA	M. CHIRIAIEFF
MLLE. MILOVANOVA	M. NIKITIN
MLLE. FREDOWA	M. MONAHOFF
MLLE. LINDOWSKA	M. TIKHOMIROFF
MLLE. ZALMANOWA	M. KURILOFF

   Ballade

   MLLS. KUHN, MATVEIVA, BEWICKE

   AND PLASKOWIECZKA

   ANNA PAVLOVA and M. NOVIKOFF

   Hungarian Czardas.

MLLE. GASHEWSKA	M. CHIRIAIEFF
MLLE. MILOVANOVA	M. NIKITIN
MLLE. FREDOWA	M. MONAHOFF
MLLE. LINDOWSKA	M. TIKHOMIROFF
MLLE. ZALMANOWA	M. KURILOFF

   Pas de Deux

   ANNA PAVLOVA AND M. NOVIKOFF

   Variation

   M. NOVIKOFF

(55)

Pavlova

Variation

ANNA PAVLOVA

Coda

Grand Finale, in which all the members of the IMPERIAL RUSSIAN BALLET will also take part.

Interval

10. Kracowiak..........................*Moszkowski*

THE MUNICIPAL ORCHESTRA

11. Songs (a) "Nymphs and Shepherds" ......*Purcell*
    (b) "At the midhour
        of Night" ⎫
    (c) "A Birthday" ⎭
    ....*Sir Fredk. Cowen*

MISS HELEN FAIRBANK

At the Piano — MR. WALFORD HYDEN

12. 'Cello Solos (a) "Minuetto"..............*Becker*
    (b) "Allegro Appassionato"
    ....*Saint-Saëns*

MR. PAULO GRUPPE

At the Piano — MR. WALFORD HYDEN

13. Redskin Dance........................*Minkus*

MLLE. KUHN

Mm. Chiriaieff, Nikitin, Monahoff
Shoubaloff, Tikhomiroff, and Kuriloff

(56)

14. Bow and Arrow Dance.............*Tschaikowski*

M. NOVIKOFF

15. *Le Cygne* (The Passing of the Swan)
(Arranged by Michael Fokine, Dress by
Bakst)..........................*Saint-Saëns*
This dance is descriptive of the last
death song of a swan. Danced to one of the
finest compositions of Saint-Saëns, it com-
mences with a plaintive melody given out
by the 'cello and harp, which instruments
form its accompaniments throughout. In
this dance one follows the movements of a
swan in perfect harmony with the strains
of the music. Gradually the movements of
the swan and the music mingle together,
and, as the swan falls to earth dead, the
music dies away.

ANNA PAVLOVA

16. Obertass (Polish Peasant Dance)....*Levandowski*

MLLE. GASHEWSKA AND M. SHOUBALOFF

17. Bohemian Dance..................

MLLE. KUHN	M. CHIRIAIEFF
MLLE. MATVEIVA	M. MONAHOFF
MLLE. BEWICKE	M. NIKITIN
MLLE. FREDOWA	M. TIKHOMIROFF
MLLE. ZALMANOWA	M. KURILOFF

Pavlova

18. Danse Bacchanale.................*Glazounow*

This dance illustrates the vivid descriptions of the revels of the Bacchantes, handed down to us by the ancient classic writers.

ANNA PAVLOVA AND M. NOVIKOFF

Musical Director: MR. THEODORE STIER

Between her two seasons in London in the year 1910, Pavlova made a quick visit to New York, where she opened at the Metropolitan Opera House on October 16th with a short season, in which she danced her ballet "Giselle." Her fame had preceded her to America and her personal appearance only increased her already great reputation. She paid several return visits to America. The American nation came to love Pavlova, and before the end of her career she had danced in every State of the Union. She was perhaps even better known there than in any other country. There has never been a theatrical star of the first magnitude who has personally appeared in as many theatres and countries as Pavlova.

In the years 1911 and 1912, she had two sea-

sons in England, including a command performance before the present King and Queen.

In January, 1913, she was in Berlin at the Kroll
Opera House with an augmented company. Here
it was that she produced Fokine's two ballets, "Les
Préludes" and "The Seven Daughters", in an attempt to achieve something distinctive in the art
of ballet itself. I recall two interesting performances
which were attended by the members of the German Royal House. The first was before Kaiser
Wilhelm. It was an established custom (of which
Pavlova knew nothing) that there should be no
applause in the theatre in the presence of the
Emperor. Pavlova was amazed and hurt when, at
the conclusion of one of her brilliant solos, the
house remained silent. Then something unpre-
cedented occurred. The Kaiser was so enthused
that he stood up in his box and applauded by himself. Within a few seconds the loyal Germans had
followed the example of their Overlord and the
theatre thundered with a tempest of cheers.

The other incident concerned the Crown Prince
(known jocularly during the War as "Little Wil-
lie"). He could not see the stage well enough
from his box. During the interval, he had the oc-

cupants of the two front rows of the stalls removed and he and his suite went and sat there in order to see as much as they possibly could.

In the year 1913, Pavlova went back to Russia, not to dance, but for a short rest. In March of the same year, she returned to London for a season, and in December she sailed for a second time to America.

In the year 1914, she danced in Hannover and Berlin (Theatre des Westens) where she had a great success with "Giselle." She then revisited Russia, this time to dance by invitation in St. Petersburg, at the Narodny Dom, and also by command at the Imperial Residence at Pavlovsk. She danced also in Moscow while on her way to the Caucasus for a short holiday.

On the date when war was declared by Russia, Pavlova was travelling through Germany on her way to London. As she was a Russian subject, she had the greatest difficulty in escaping from Germany, and but for the merest of accidents she might have been destined to remain interned throughout the whole of the War period. She managed to get through, but all her luggage and personal effects were detained in Germany. She was

Pavlova

at her home in London when war was declared by Great Britain. She did not know what to do or how she could help. Under a previously made engagement she sailed for America in September, 1914.

I did not accompany Pavlova to America, and it was not until after the War that I resumed my relationship with her. For any facts relating to her experiences during this period I have had to rely on my memory of what she herself and other members of the Company have told me at various times. I conclude this chapter with a brief categorical outline of the rest of her career as a world figure.

After a winter season in New York, she went in May, 1915, to California for a rest. Early in 1916 she was again in New York, where she danced at the Century Theatre. In March of that year, she began a tour through Havana, Panama, Chili, Peru, the Argentine, and Brazil.

She spent Christmas, 1916, at Porto Rico where, to the amusement of the people staying at her hotel, she insisted upon having a Christmas tree with the traditional Russian snow settings — in the midst of an intense heat wave.

She was at Costa Rica in March, 1917, when the

(61)

news came of the Russian Revolution (Kerensky's *coup d'état*).

Throughout the whole of this Latin-American tour she was everywhere rapturously received. In Peru, after her performance of "Giselle", not only was the stage covered with flowers, but pigeons were released to fly in the theatre and on the stage — to the unbounded delight of Pavlova herself who loved birds almost more than anything else in her life. In Venezuela she was presented with a velvet jewel case on the cover of which her name was emblazoned in gold coins.

In 1918 she finished her South American tour and began a season in Mexico. Here her reception was greater than in any other country she visited. Instead of staying two weeks, as originally planned, she remained for eight weeks. Every Sunday she danced in the Bull Ring before an audience of thirty-six thousand people. She also danced in what are known as the middle-class theatres, where fathers of families bring their wives and children — an audience not less demonstrative than that of the Bull Ring, even if smaller in number.

In 1921 she danced in London at Drury Lane. She left immediately for the United States of

America, where for seven months she played in one hundred and forty towns. She had a special train in which the Company lived during their periods of prolonged travelling between perform-ances.

The following year (1922) she was back in London at Covent Garden in May; and revisited Paris in July. In the autumn of this year she started out on a tour to Japan via Canada. This was her first visit to the Oriental World. Her reception by the Japanese was no less enthusiastic than that to which she had become accustomed elsewhere.

There were very few Westernised theatres in Japan, and Pavlova not only danced in these, but also in the Japanese theatres in the provincial towns. The Japanese excelled themselves in hospitality. I pause here to narrate a curious incident which shows that one should not always take offers of hospitality too lightly. Pavlova was asked what she would like to eat, her Japanese host adding that there was nothing grown on land or in the water, no fish, flesh or fowl, which he would not be happy to procure for her delight. Pavlova wistfully ex-pressed her desire for mushrooms. Either this vege-table is rare in Japan or else it was the wrong season; but her host had to spend thousands of yen in order to procure a small quantity of them. To make matters worse, the Japanese cook had no idea how the dainty should be prepared in the Russian manner, which is what Pavlova had stipulated. In despair they approached Pavlova's trusted henchman and factotum, Kusma, and told him their difficulty. Delighted, he prepared the dish for Madame. Unfortunately, the mushrooms turned out to be of the poisonous variety, and the whole procedure of obtaining new ones had to be gone through again. In the end, Pavlova got her mushrooms. When she realized to what trouble her host had been put, she was overwhelmed with confusion.

It was while she was on this tour that Pavlova made the notes for the first number of the ballet "Oriental Impressions." She danced for a time in the rôle of the Japanese dancer in this number but later abandoned it and assigned the rôle to one of her principal dancers.

After leaving Japan, the Company journeyed to India, stopping at Shanghai on the way. Here Pavlova was sickened by seeing a policeman beat a coolie upon the head until he fell senseless, and

PAVLOVA'S DRESSING ROOM, COVENT GARDEN

she swore she would never visit such a brutal place again. She had purchased some shawls which she promptly gave away, in order not to retain any memory of the experience.

On arrival in India, where she danced before the Viceroy, she made additional notes for her ballet "Oriental Impressions." As I am merely giving her world itinerary here, I must leave some descriptions of incidental experiences until a later chapter.

From India she travelled to Egypt, where she danced in Cairo, after spending a night alone in the desert in front of the Sphinx. At Alexandria, the Russian refugees subscribed for and presented her with a sumptuous basket of flowers. Pavlova was dismayed and unhappy because she knew that the refugees had spent their last money to honour her. In autumn 1923, after a brief holiday in Italy, she reappeared in London at Covent Garden.

The following year she revisited New York, California and Mexico. In 1925, she was back in London, after which she played short seasons in Germany and Paris before leaving for South Africa. It was on this trip that Pavlova achieved her greatest *tour de force* in producing a Russian Christmas tree on board ship — at the Equator!

From South Africa she travelled to Australia, where she met Chaliapin and the Don Cossack Choir. After touring for thousands of miles in every State of that continent, she went to New Zealand, and was back again in Germany by the end of 1926.

The following year she began an extended English tour with a season at Covent Garden. In a later chapter, I give the itinerary of this tour, showing how in ten weeks we gave eighty performances in more than fifty theatres. She then went to Holland, Germany, Switzerland, Italy and Paris, before leaving for South America in June, 1928.

She was back again in London in September of the same year, and at once set out on her Eastern tour through Egypt, India, Burma, the Straits Settlements, Java, and Australia, to return home in August, 1929. After a short vacation at Ivy House, she toured through Spain, Switzerland, Czecho-Slovakia, Denmark, Sweden, Norway, to finish at Hamburg and Paris.

In the year 1930 her last tour began. Although

she had an injured kneecap, she danced once more through the English provinces, to appear in public for the last time in her career, on the 13th of December 1930, at the Golders Green Hippodrome, almost at the gates of her home. She had arranged another prolonged Continental tour to begin in Holland, after a short rest in the South of France, where she intended to have treatment for her injured knee.

But she never got farther than Holland. When travelling from the South of France in January she contracted a chill which resulted in her death after she had reached The Hague.

She died on tour.

CHAPTER IV

Ivy House

ANNA PAVLOVA made the world her country and London her home. Ivy House, at Hampstead, formed an ideal background for her. It was a house which used to belong to Turner the painter. She once expressed to me a naïve pleasure in this fact. She said, "I am glad to be living in a house that used to belong to an artist!" Not because Turner was Turner, be it noted, but because Turner was *an artist!*

The house stands in beautiful gardens. On a lake which was excavated to Pavlova's design there were swans. Anna Pavlova loved her swans. She was quite unafraid of them, would seize them rapturously and play with them by the water's edge for hours. There was no affectation in this. Despite the fact that she had danced "The Swan" dance innumerable times, she never allowed herself to become self-conscious in her love for the birds themselves. The birds never injured her in any way. They knew her when she called them and would submit to her fondling and to her rough handling without a sign of fear. It was not so much a pretty sight as an astonishing sight to watch her with her swans. She *romped* with them. She would tease them, try to irritate them, push them and pull them roughly, abuse them boisterously, roll on the grass with them, like a high-spirited boy playing with a spaniel. And the swans would take on an almost human expression — not of anger, but of cunning pleasure. She would let them caress her face with their strong beaks. Surely there has never been anything quite like this since Jove paid his respects to Leda!

As well as the swans, she had flamingoes and a peacock. It was amusing, when lunching with her, to see this peacock come to the open French window and display his tail, asking for titbits. She was inordinately fond of birds and had an aviary in the grounds of Ivy House stocked with these little creatures of the air, collected by her on her travels in every part of the world. She would feed them and clean them herself. Her affinity with birds was one of the most revealing and noteworthy of her qualities, despite the fact that it was what might have been expected.

She loved flowers and all growing things. In summer she would be up early, when at home, out in the garden digging and transplanting flowers. She revelled in the earth's power to transmit life to plants. She preferred the country to the town and sometimes she would express a wistful desire to be away from the bustle and rush of theatrical life, to live peacefully in some country cottage. In particular, she loved the English countryside, and often she said she wished she had a chance to know it more intimately than she did. She would say, when worried, "I wish I could go into the *deep* country and rest with God."

Many people will remember the "House-warming" Garden Party given by Pavlova at Ivy House in 1910. The leaders of society and fashion were present. Foreign ambassadors and the élite of the English aristocracy were pleased to accept the invitation of the exquisite Russian ballerina whose dancing was the talk of London. By an oversight, Mrs. Asquith (now Lady Oxford) was not included in the first list of invitations, but the omission was discovered just in time. Afterwards, Mrs.

IVY HOUSE, HAMPSTEAD, LONDON

Pavlova

Asquith wrote to Pavlova, expressing her pleasure at having been present, and I remember Pavlova saying how glad she was that the invitation had not been overlooked!

On the lawns at Ivy House, she moved among her guests like the incarnation of youthful loveliness and grace. She had engaged the orchestra of the Palace Theatre for the occasion, and the guests were entertained by various theatrical artists, among whom I remember particularly Albert Whelan, the Australian singer. Suddenly, from behind the shrubs, there emerged a ballet of little girls dancing a *pastorale* designed by Pavlova for the occasion. She had taken trouble in training these children, and the guests were entranced by an effect which, under that gentle summer sky, was nothing less than idyllic. To crown everything, Pavlova herself danced as a shepherdess. She seemed to belong to another world. Before the blasé society people, she appeared as a vision of perfection in rhythm and lightness, like a creature come freshly to life from Watteau's paintings, or like a goddess from the ancient Elysium.

There was another charming garden party about this time — a Theatrical Garden Party in aid of charity. Pavlova was selling copies of a new waltz by Hermann Finck (then musical director at the Palace Theatre) which had been composed for the occasion. While I was playing the piece over on the piano in the "Anna Pavlova" tent, she was selling the copies at the price marked. She would autograph copies on request, leaving the extra price to the discretion of the purchaser. But if a golden sovereign was tendered, Anna Pavlova did not understand enough English to give change! Without saying a word, she would shrug her shoulders prettily, there would be a chink of gold in the cash box and a flash of sparkling black eyes. That was the only change — in this good cause.

On this occasion, a shy young girl came to Pavlova and asked for her autograph on a copy of the piece by Hermann Finck which she was selling. The girl made it clear that she could not afford to pay extra for the autograph, so Pavlova opened her own purse and dropped a sovereign in the box. More than a year later, the same girl came to an audition before Pavlova and was at once recognized, though their previous encounter had lasted only a few seconds in a crowded afternoon.

That was characteristic of her. She was naturally charming, despite the occasional outbursts of ugly temper of which she was capable when worried by her work. At Ivy House she lived quietly. She was not addicted to entertaining, though when she did entertain she was the perfect hostess, making each guest feel like the guest of honour, never neglecting the intimate observances of social tact and personal taste. She had the makings of an ideal wife and mother — this high priestess whose sacrifice was herself; but because she had devoted her life to an object which she considered holy, the lesser pleasures which normal women enjoy were denied to her. Her home was only a place to which she could go on vacations — and her vacations were not rests; they were periods of preparation for more work.

She had a dancing studio at Ivy House and, in her earliest days there, she had a small School of Ballet for young girls. It was in this way that she hoped to form the nucleus of her Company for the later world tours. However, she had to abandon this idea because she was never at Ivy House long enough at one time to complete the regular training of her own girls.

She selected members of her *corps-de-ballet* for

her world tours through the ordinary theatrical channels. Although she preferred Russian dancers, because, as she put it, of their "mystic" quality, it was surprising as time went on how many English and American girls she included, sometimes under Russian names, in her *corps-de-ballet*. She also had girls of other nationalities: Danish, Polish, Roumanian, German, Italian, Czecho-Slovakian. No matter what training these girls had received before joining her Ballet, Pavlova considered it incumbent upon her to make them conform to her own ideas of style and technique. In this way, and in others, the Pavlova Ballet was a creation of Pavlova and not merely a collection of theatrical performers. The members of the Ballet were her creatures, used by her for a purpose which she managed to make them feel was transcendental.

About three hundred dancers in all in the twenty-two years of her life outside Russia can claim to have had the experience of dancing with her. I should mention that she recruited many of her girls from the schools established in Paris, after the Revolution, by the Russian ballerinas, Egorova, Trefilova, and Preobrajenskaya. Whenever she went to Paris she called and paid her respects at their studios, with a charmingly un-selfconscious modesty and deference.

An amusing story is told of a visit by Pavlova to Madame Egorova's School. She was sitting with some others watching some of Egorova's pupils dance. Seated next to Pavlova was an unduly large matron, whose daughter was one of the pupils about to dance. Not knowing who Pavlova was, the fond mother asked her if she knew anything about dancing. Pavlova replied "A little." The mother went on, "Well, you will know a lot more after you have seen my daughter dance. She is absolutely a genius. She is easily the best pupil here. I fully expect that in a few years she will be a greater dancer than Pavlova!" To this Pavlova answered very calmly, "Do you really think so? Have you ever seen Pavlova dance?" The mother looked scornfully at her. "Seen her dance!" she exclaimed. "Why, it was Madame Pavlova herself who told me that my daughter will become one of the greatest dancers in the world!"

At this point, while Pavlova was trying to decide whether to become indignant or to burst out in laughter, Madame Egorova brought her pupil forward and presented her to — Madame Pavlova.

Pavlova

The boastful matron, on hearing the name, did her best to sink through the floor before making a hurried and indecorous exit.

In Pavlova's studio at Ivy House, there were handrails all along one side of the room and a very big mirror taking up most of the wall space opposite. On the parquet floor, Pavlova loved to do her exercises, whirling and posing as she watched herself in the mirror, always anxious to see if there were any possible method of improving her technique. In one corner of the room was a grand piano, which had been presented to her in America. On the walls were drawings by Bakst and a portrait of Taglione. Framed with this print was a piece of ribbon which had been used by Taglione when dancing the part of Giselle.

When Pavlova happened to be in London for Christmas, it was in this room that she gave her Christmas parties. There was a balcony in the room which would be festooned with streamers, and on tables around the walls there would be every kind of wine to which the guests might help themselves. At the rehearsal of "La Fille Mal Gardée", after the first London performance in 1910, already mentioned, something happened which will cause me to remember this room forever. After we had been rehearsing all night, the pale dawn came in at the windows, and I, for one — having been at the piano without rest for eighteen hours: at the day rehearsal, the evening performance, and the all-night rehearsal — had a splitting headache. To cheer me up, Pavlova brought a full tumbler of real pre-War vodka, which in my then state of innocence, I took for water and tossed off at a gulp. The subsequent proceedings interested me no more!

The amount of time given by Pavlova to practising was one explanation of her perfection of technique. In one sense, she never stopped practising. Even when she was talking to people or when she was supposed to be taking a rest, her fingers would be moving, or her limbs. She seemed utterly incapable of resting or standing still. When at home, she spent at least three hours in the morning practising by herself in her studio. Afterwards she would go out into the grounds and play with her swans by the lake.

I feel sad when I think of Pavlova at Ivy House. She was happy there, but she had so little time to enjoy the happiness which a home gives to the wanderer. She was a wanderer always, it seemed, under some fierce compulsion to go out into the world, away from a beautiful home she loved, away from comforts, to the worrying routine of work and the discomfort of perpetual travel.

Her life was so full of work that she never had time to do what she wanted, other than to dance, for she wanted to dance most of all. Thus she always intended to write her memoirs and always she had to put it off until later. Now, because of her unexpected death, the world will never know her own impressions and reflections on an exceptionally brilliant and many-sided life.

I know, in the main, what she would have written, for she expressed it verbally often enough. For her, life had no meaning except as an art-expression, and the highest form of art was the classical dance. Without the impulse to this expression, Pavlova could not have lived. She used to say "Art is not a flower of leisure or a relaxation. Art means work. It is useless to dabble in beauty. One must be utterly devoted to beauty with every nerve in the body."

No doubt she was right. It is possible to climb part way up the mountain of artistic endeavour without undue exertion, but those who would reach the topmost peaks must be prepared for arduous toil. Pavlova had a curious little saying to express this: "Those who wish to achieve great things in art have no time to *cross the hands*."

Her outlook on life was simple and it was real. She was never in a fantasy of dream. She was always practical. Thanks to a native quick intelligence, she could soon sum up a position and value people at their worth. I do not think that she could ever have lost her head in an emergency.

She attracted thousands of people, not only by her genius as a dancer, but by her individual and essential charm, which was hypnotic in its effect. The multitudes who did not know her personally have admired her in her art; but those who knew her well, besides admiring her work, found her a unique creature. Celebrities of all nations, statesmen, artists, men of spirit, of thought, and of talent, found a most particular satisfaction in exchanging even a few words with her. She left the feeling of enchantment, which only a delightful personality can convey in a few moments of conversation.

Though in practical matters she was so efficient and realistic, one felt all the time that she was unreal, superhuman. She asked nothing for herself. She was in private life a most unostentatious person. She thought only of her work. Few people knew how good-hearted she was, always ready to help in private and public charities and never asking any thanks or reward other than the satisfaction which she herself felt in helping where aid was needed.

Thus her life at Ivy House was as quiet and restful as the demands of her work allowed it to be. On her wanderings she liked to think of her home, to look at photographs of the garden, to wonder how things were growing, and whether the birds were being properly cared for. She liked to think that she was a woman with a home to go to, where she could retire from the strenuousness of a life in public. And the pathos is that for all her wistful love of home, she was scarcely ever there for more than a few fleeting weeks at a time.

She had a hobby which should be mentioned, because it throws a light on her character as well as on her work. She was fond of sculpture. Greek sculpture gave her the keenest pleasure. She was a connoisseur in the ancient bas-reliefs and frescoes portraying dancing mænads, and when examining them unconsciously fell into the pose depicted before her.

In her periods of "leisure" at Ivy House, she modelled in wax and clay, and the results were interesting as an example of her absorption in her own art of dancing. She made little female figures, nude and draped. The effect was delightful, but Pavlova was never satisfied. After her figures had been "fired", and she saw the completed glazed effect, she wanted to make alterations, and this being impossible she would promptly set to work to create a new figure. Whatever may have been the artistic value of her little statues, they were correct in poise and the dancing gesture, which is more than can be said for many attempts at dancing figures made by professional plastic artists. It was amazing how, although untutored, she was able to convey the effect of rhythmical movement in these little creations of clay. I understand that some of her dancing figures were bought by a firm of art dealers, who had reproductions made which are on sale in art shops to this day.

Pavlova was not ostentatious in her dress. She never tried to attract attention to herself by any form of loudness in attire or jewelry. To those acquainted with the vanity of theatrical "stars" this point throws a light on her character. She was modest in appearance when in street or travelling dress. The temptation to make herself look exotic she resisted, though nothing would have been easier had she cared to strive for this effect. The truth is that Anna Pavlova had the innate modesty and restraint of a true artist. She had no need to strive for "effect", and she had no desire to attract attention to herself in a social gathering.

This does not mean that she dressed plainly. She dressed simply, which is another matter. Neither does it mean that she dressed cheaply. I have it on the best authority that she never visited Paris without spending at least one hundred thousand francs in one of the *maisons-de-couture*. As why should she not?

As a touch of adornment she wore earrings, which conveyed a refined gypsy effect. She was fond of wearing on her finger a ring set with a Queensland black opal, a curious stone with dark iridescent effects, which had been presented to her by Australian admirers. That stone was something like Pavlova's own mystical Russian soul — dark and iridescent.

Pavlova

She had hundreds of pairs of shoes. Incidentally, her ballet shoes were made specially to her order, and she always had dozens of pairs in use simultaneously. She would "break in" a new pair gradually at rehearsals. The care of her feet was of supreme importance. Her feet were most sensitive to touch impressions. They were like a marvellously delicate instrument, a diaphragm of nerves.

She dieted carefully. She liked fish, olives, plain foods; and without being a faddist she ate only what would enable her to keep fit for work. If she found herself a pound or two overweight, she would double the amount of her exercising and fast until she was the right weight once more. She never indulged herself. She was more than human.

Among the visitors at Ivy House, there was one whose visit must be considered as an historical event. In 1913, Saint-Saëns visited Anna Pavlova at her home, and played several of his compositions to her, to see if any other piece than "Le Cygne" could be adapted to her dancing. Nothing appealed to her as did "Le Cygne." In all her career she only danced one other composition of his — the Syrian Dance from "Samson and Delilah." I was young in the musical world then, and I was deeply impressed by the dignity of the venerable composer, white-haired and white-bearded, in strong contrast with the vivacious, dark-eyed, excitable young Russian, gay and so very sure of herself.

I asked her afterwards what she really thought of the music of Saint-Saëns. She merely replied that the man himself emitted a shining light! This was the kind of answer one had to expect from Pavlova. She had all kinds of "psychic" intuitions into the character of people she met. People were luminous or non-luminous to her. I have heard her boast that she could "see through" people as through a glass.

The impression I had of this meeting was that both Pavlova and Saint-Saëns realized that their partnership, if it could be called that, in "The Swan" was not likely to be bettered in any other composition of his. He told her frankly that he was astonished at the strength and beauty of her creation and Pavlova looked at him in amazement. She was inclined to venerate other people of genius and with sincere modesty to decry her own achievement. She told Saint-Saëns that once in Russia, when she was very young, she called upon Glazounow by arrangement. She was terrified that the

PAVLOVA IN THE SWAN DANCE

redoubtable composer would prove an ogre; but he proved quite otherwise. He composed a special piece for Anna Pavlova, and this she danced in the Mariansky Theatre — though she never included it in her later repertoires.

In the early days of her triumph, at the first performance of "The Three Palms" at the Kroll Opera House in Berlin, Nikitsch and Richard Strauss came to her dressing room after the performance. It was interesting to observe that while Strauss thanked her in a few well-chosen words for the pleasure she had given him, Nikitsch became rhapsodical in his adulation, so greatly had she moved him by her art. Pavlova was elated at the homage of such giants, but as the years went by and she became a world figure, she received calmly enough the personal homage of almost every one of distinction on the earth. Kings and queens were frequently in her audiences but no matter how exalted the admirers of her art, she was not unduly flattered or impressed. She would dance as well for a beggar as for a prince. She had met the world's leading scientists, artists, inventors, philosophers, musicians, and people who matter, but once she said to me very sadly, "I meet so many interesting people, but I never get time to know anybody at all!"

This is the tragedy of all theatrical life and Pavlova had the intelligence to know that it was her own tragedy. Wherever she went, she was the focus of intense activity. Leading citizens and people of no intrinsic importance persistently sent their cards to her dressing room. She could hardly refuse to see them without conveying an unnecessary affront. And often these functionaries of local importance grimaced and postured before her, giving themselves the airs of people really worth something. Pavlova would have to be patient with them, open their tawdry bazaars for them, even watch their only-too-awkward daughters attempt to dance for her praise! She was so quick to friendship with real people — so pestered with people of no importance. People would never leave her alone, but always she was lonely. No wonder, then, that on her periodical returns home to Ivy House, she drew a deep breath and tried to become a woman with her own household things about her and her own flowers and birds in the garden.

Anna Pavlova's mother has paid a visit to Ivy House. I did not have the pleasure of meeting this lady, but Pavlova has shown me a photograph of her mother taken in the grounds of Ivy House, and she told me at the same time that her mother had to return to Russia because she was the holder of a Soviet passport. Anna Pavlova's mother is still living in Russia, and I cannot help thinking it must have been a wonderful experience for her to visit the beautiful London home of her world-famous daughter and to be reminded of the time when her little Nura had pestered her to be allowed to enter the Imperial School.

At home Pavlova had typical Russian habits. For instance, she liked what is known as "Russian" tea, or tea with a slice of lemon, sipped for hours during conversation. She was very serious in her devotion to the orthodox Russian religion. On tour she attended services in towns where there was a Russian Church. She had a little holy image (ikon) which accompanied her everywhere and was placed by her bedside, even in ships' cabins and railway berths. Before each performance she would make the Sign of the Cross, and sometimes before her entry for "The Swan."

She observed scrupulously the festivals of Easter and Christmas. At Easter she would give a party to the Russian members of the Company, with the traditional Easter cakes. At Christmas, no matter where we were — even at sea — she had a Christmas tree, hung with gifts. She always remembered the "name" days of Russian members of her Company and would congratulate them and give them little presents.

Incidentally, while she was addressed as "Madame" by all nationalities other than Russian, she was invariably addressed directly as "Anna Pavlova" by the Russians. The Russian communities everywhere loved her, exiles and Bolsheviks. She received shortly before her death an impressive illuminated scroll from Moscow, signed by all the members of the Moscow Art Theatre, paying tribute to her great achievements.

Each time she had to leave her home on one of her prolonged world tours, she would go into every room and say good-bye to her favourite household objects, then out in the garden to say good-bye to her birds and flowers. When she would come back into the drawing-room she would be weeping. She would sit on a chair and pray, blessing her home in the Russian manner before leaving it. She never failed to observe this ritual — except

once. This was on the last occasion when she left
Ivy House on her departure for the Continental
tour during which she died. When leaving the
house this time, she astonished everybody by her
hurry. She seemed to be running blindly away
from the home she was never to see again.

CHAPTER V

On Tour

WHEN Pavlova took her Ballet Company on
tour she was the commander in chief of a small
army.

There would be twenty-two ballet girls, besides
two principal dancers (one a character dancer) —
and Pavlova. There would be a dozen male dancers, including two principals, one of them her partner, the other her *maître de ballet*. This constituted
a *corps-de-ballet* of nearly forty dancers of all nationalities — but with many traits in common,
including, chiefly, a devotion to the dance, and an
adoration of the Goddess of Dance, as personified
in Pavlova.

Besides her musical director, a small orchestra
travelled at times with the company. At other times
she would have only a trio, consisting of violinist,
'cellist and pianist. These three executants formed
the nucleus for an orchestra with whatever other

musical material the various theatres provided. For some time the Cherniavsky trio travelled in this capacity with Pavlova's Company.

A stage manager, an electrician, a librarian, a wig man, three stage hands and supernumeraries were indispensable. Pavlova's maid, and as many as five wardrobe mistresses (three for the women, and two for the men) completed the tally — with the exception of one very important personage not yet mentioned, Monsieur Victor Dandré, Pavlova's husband and business manager, and general manager of the whole concern, as Pavlova was its inspiration.

It would be easy to write an entire book of travel describing places and things seen by the Pavlova Company, and it would require another full-sized volume to detail the organization necessary for arranging such a tour in its business and practical aspects. But the reader of this book must be left to imagine the amount of activity involved in transporting her Company to every part of the globe, and the reader must imagine, or consult other books for, descriptions of picturesque places and peoples encountered in an itinerary which included every town of importance in the world. I write of Pavlova, not of the people and places and things which any one can visit, with or without a theatrical company.

It was the Pavlova Ballet, not only in name, but in fact. In every dispute, in any difficulty or any untoward contingency, Madame's decision was final. She was not merely a theatrical star engaged for a tour under the management of impressarios who took all responsibility for her. She was her own manager, her own financier. Monsieur Dandré was a rock of steadiness to her in all practical matters and relieved her of much worry, but there was nothing crucial relating to the organization of the Company which could be decided without Pavlova's application to it.

Often her quick intuition would give an immediate decision on anything from the planning of an itinerary to the emergency repairing of a piece of scenery, or a sudden alteration in the programme.

Not only was the Company dependent upon her for its morale and its inspiration in the work itself, but also in those multifarious details involved in the transporting of an æsthetic army to every quarter of the globe — a missionary and spiritual enterprise, as she conceived it.

Pavlova

I shall describe in a later chapter how the ballets were rehearsed and performed. For the moment, I ask the reader merely to bear in mind that wherever we went, visiting new theatres, there had to be strenuous rehearsals before the performance could take place, and that there were a thousand and one distractions from the work to which the Company was consecrated.

The Company travelled quickly. Tours were organized at a high pressure. Tons of scenery, costumes, and properties, besides the personnel, had to be rushed hither and thither, from town to town, always in a race against time. Everywhere Pavlova arrived with a violent impact and departed like a storm gust. The curtain had to go up at a certain time. That was a law of nature. Everything had to conform to this law. How few members of our audiences, sitting comfortably in their reserved seats after a good dinner, looking forward to an evening's entertainment, could have given even a passing thought to the rush and bustle and concentrated fury of preparation which had preceded the opening bars of the overture!

To show the speed at which the Company travelled, I give below the itinerary of our English provincial tour of 1927. The tour began on October 3d and ended on December 10th.

First Week: Margate, Folkestone, Hastings, Brighton, Eastbourne, Shanklin (Isle of Wight), Bournemouth.

Second Week: Leicester, Nottingham, Derby, Sheffield, Leeds, Halifax.

Third Week: Huddersfield, Bradford, Blackburn, Llandudno, Hanley.

Fourth Week: Manchester, Warrington, Liverpool, Preston.

Fifth Week: Birmingham.

Sixth Week: Glasgow, Dundee, Aberdeen, Perth, Edinburgh.

Seventh Week: Newcastle, Middlesborough, West Hartlepool, Darlington, York, Hull.

Eighth Week: Newark, Oxford, Portsmouth, Bournemouth.

Ninth Week: Bristol, Cardiff, Swansea, Plymouth, Torquay, Exeter.

Tenth Week: Cheltenham, Kidderminster, Worcester, Rugby.

Pavlova

To cast an eye over this itinerary gives some idea
of the speed at which the ground was covered. It
will be noticed that during the first week, for example, there were seven towns visited in six days.
This is because we played a matinée on Thursday
afternoon at Brighton and the evening performance at Eastbourne. In the ten weeks of the tour,
eighty performances were given, matinées included, in fifty theatres. Before each performance,
a rehearsal had to take place, as the Company
had to get used to the stage and the theatre, and
the orchestra also required to be drilled in the
music.

It may be imagined that after such an amount
of work and travel, there would be a period of rest
and recuperation. There was — exactly three days!
After that, the company travelled to Holland and
played at The Hague and Rotterdam, arriving at
Amsterdam for Christmas week. A tour through
Holland followed, mostly one-night "stands", and
January 25th found us in Cologne. Before the end
of that week we had visited Dortmund, Munster,
Kassel, Erfurt.

During February, we visited Leipzig, Halle,
Magdeburg, Dresden, Aussig, Zittau, Reichen-

berg, Leignitz, Gorlitz, Breslau, Gleiwitz, Beu-
then, Chemnitz, Bamberg, Nuremberg, Munich.

In March, after a season of five nights at Munich,
we went on to Ulm, Frankfort, Darmstadt, Mann-
heim, Wiesbaden, Pforsheim, Stuttgart, Freiburg,
Basle and Zurich.

April found us in Italy where we played at
Milan, Genoa, Turin, Parma, Florence and Rome,
to end that particular tour with a season in Paris in
May. After a vacation of only one month, the Company sailed for South America on June 24th. During the month's rest at Ivy House, Pavlova was re-
arranging the Company's repertoire, rehearsing
new ballets, overhauling the costumes and settings,
and so on.

The catalogue of places and dates which I have
given above shows merely the amount of ground
which she covered in one specimen year of her life
of touring. Immediately after the return from
South America, she was off again, eastwards this
time, to Egypt, India, Burma, Singapore, Java
and Australia. . . .

She was probably the most travelled woman in
the world. In America she danced in almost every
city of any size and certainly in every State —

enough travelling for a lifetime for most people. But Pavlova had been everywhere else besides.

Travelling was so much a part of her life that after the shortest of vacations at home, much as she loved Ivy House, she was invariably eager to set out again on her journeyings, particularly if the itinerary included a country which she had not previously visited. But there were few countries she had not visited. On her last tour to the East she could not conceal her delight when we were nearing Java, a country in which she had not previously danced. As the boat neared Java, I was strolling up and down the deck with her when she said, in that impetuous way of hers, "I think the girls" (*i.e.* the girls in the Company) "will like to see Java. We may not do good business there, but I have heard so much about it, and I am so interested to see it, that I do not mind about business. We shall forget money, for once. Let us see a beautiful country we have not ever seen before."

When we reached Java, Pavlova was delighted with the exotic scenery. She said, "It is like a *décor* by Bakst!"

But what the rest of the Company will remember more than anything else is the terrific heat. It was not the dry heat of Port Sudan or of Townsville in North Australia. It was a damp, sticky, and clammy heat. The dancers in the ballet could not keep their "make-up" on. Every one was bathed in perspiration. All the Company complained of this peculiar heat, which made them feel so limp. All except one! The intense heat did not seem to effect Pavlova. She thrived on it. She was fresh for each performance. She continued her unremitting practice; and when the other members of the Company complained of the heat, she replied, "Yes. It is so nice to have it warm like this. It is so much easier to dance."

That was Pavlova. If we had been at the North Pole, she would have said that the climate was admirably suited to dancing because of its exhilarating coldness which compelled one to move quickly.

In Java, the entire Company was invited to a native performance which took place in an open-air theatre. I mention the incident here to show the kind of ordeal which was, alas, only too considerable a feature of Pavlova's life when on tour — the ordeal of submitting to well-intentioned efforts to please her. At this performance there were about a dozen dancers in grotesque costumes and masks.

Pavlova

The orchestra consisted of five players, — three upon an instrument which resembled a huge xylophone comprising only five notes, and two Javanese drums. The dancing went on for five hours without any interludes, the "ballet" posturing and using their arms in an extraordinarily angular — in fact, a distorted — way. All the time the industrious members of the "orchestra" were beating out their monotonous notes until we almost lost our reason and could have screamed and rushed from the place, but for politeness. Perhaps the intention of the performance was to make the audience lose their reason and submit to primitive emotions. We almost succumbed!

Wherever she went, she was more interested in the daily lives of the people than in the "show" places of the usual tourist itinerary. In particular, she wanted to know how the poor people lived. In the East she was appalled by the poverty and misery of the lowest classes. She thought it incredible that human beings could exist at all in such circumstances. Then she would say, "But what can be done to help? It is so vast, this misery, it extends everywhere." She would become sad because she herself could do nothing to help.

Pavlova

I shall never forget the picture of Anna Pavlova crooning, as she fondled two dark-skinned babies in India, whom she found in a village street sitting in the dust, as naked as when they were born. The children got over their shyness as they played with the fairy princess who had come into their lives, a creature from the child's world of fantasy. Though she could not speak their language, nor they hers, Pavlova gave an expression to her gentlest and most deep emotions of mother-love. When she had to leave them, she looked back time and again, and I noticed that there were real tears in her eyes.

She had no children of her own. She often expressed the wish that she had, but she had sacrificed her life, she told me, for her art alone. But I have heard it said that she was physiologically incapable of bearing children. The story goes that the Russian doctor who first told her this, said, "God has made you for a purpose that is greater than giving birth to children."

Yet she understood and loved children and they loved her. A well-meaning woman in one of the towns we visited — the wife of a civic potentate — managed to secure admission to Pavlova's dressing

PAVLOVA IN THE RUSSIAN DANCE WHICH SHE REVIVED AT
THE METROPOLITAN OPERA HOUSE

room after a performance. The fond mother had brought her little girl, aged six, to present a bouquet to Madame. As the child shyly held out the flowers, Pavlova bent down and kissed her. Then she stood erect, her eyes blazing with fury, and spoke to the mother. "How dare you!" she said. "how dare you bring such a tiny child to me *at midnight?* She should have been in her bed long ago!" The mother looked at her in amazement. Pavlova stamped her foot on the floor in a rage. "Go!" she almost screamed. "Take the little one away to bed. Her eyes can scarcely open!" The abashed mother could find nothing to say in reply to this unexpected but well-merited rebuke.

A noteworthy example of her maternal impulse is the fact that wherever we went through the world, all proceeds of sales of Pavlova's photographs were set aside for a charity of her own. This was a Home for Russian Children in Paris. She established this hostel and contributed liberally to it from her private bank account.

No doubt it was a sublimation of her maternal instinct which made Pavlova continually refer to her Company as "one big family." She "fussed" a great deal about the welfare of the members of the

Company on tour. If she saw a girl sitting on a deck
in the chill of evening without a wrap, Pavlova
would go up to her and tell her not to catch cold;
or again, if she heard that one of the girls had a
headache, Pavlova would send her own maid with
aspirins to the sufferer.

There may have been something more than maternal solicitude in such actions. It is obvious
enough that the whole Company had to be in the
best of health in order to do the work which Madame expected of them. Yet she managed to convey by thousands of little kindnesses that each
member of the Company was very dear to her personally. She took a maternal interest in the girls
and the girls did not resent it. If any members of
the Company fell ill, Madame would insist upon
treatment in the best hospitals or nursing homes
available. She would not allow the invalid to dance
until recovery was complete.

Incidentally, Anna Pavlova always thought of
the hospitals wherever she went. She would send
them the flowers from her bouquets, a little act of
thoughtfulness which has made her many friends
in unexpected places all over the world.

She was indeed spontaneously generous. She

hardly ever failed to give a handsome present to any one of her Company who happened to be leaving her, as a tangible souvenir of the days with Pavlova.

Because of her known generosity, she was constantly imposed upon by the writers of begging letters. Women would write to her representing themselves as having been "well-known" theatrical dancers, and then would follow the tale of woe — illness, misfortune, and so on — the letters winding up with a peroration appealing to the great heart of Pavlova for assistance, which would enable the sufferer to be relieved and to get a fresh start in life again, and so on. Pavlova did not seem to have the ability to see through this swindle, no matter how often it was practised upon her. She would send a five-pound note, or even a larger sum to particularly plausible writers, and in reply to remonstrances would only say, "Yes, it may be a fraud, but then on the other hand it may happen to be a genuine case, and I would never forgive myself for allowing some one genuinely in need to apply to me in vain!"

This woman Pavlova was an enigma. The more one thinks about her character, the more one realizes how contradictory it was in many respects. I have mentioned her solicitude for members of the Company. Yet other incidents occur to memory which can be interpreted equally as callousness. For example, only the principals of the Company travelled first class. This was not such a terrible thing in England. But in some Continental countries, and also in the East, it was not anything less than a disgrace that a trivial economy should have been effected at the expense of the comfort of the girls who spent most of their lives travelling between the periods of work in which Pavlova demanded from them the highest standard of excellence. This false economy led her into a nasty situation when we were in the East. An influential English resident almost exploded with indignation when he saw that Pavlova expected the white girls of her Company to travel second class with the natives. So insistent was he upon the girls travelling first class, and such weight did he bring to bear upon his argument, that there and then the girls were ushered into first-class compartments, and travelled so during the remainder of the tour. When she realized that she was in the wrong, Pavlova gave way.

Pavlova

I mention the foregoing incident because the reader of this book has the right to know what was unpleasant about Pavlova, though, in the last resort, such aspects of her nature do not detract from her incomparable artistic achievement. But there can be no denying that in many ways she was selfish. While making an extravagant fuss about the welfare of the Company, she by no means paid lavish salaries. When it is considered that the girls in the *corps-de-ballet* had to pay from their wages all their own hotel bills and taxi fares, and to purchase and continually renew their tights and ballet shoes, it will be realized that on a strenuous tour such expenses mount up very considerably indeed. Pavlova is reported herself to have made a large fortune, and as I am telling in this book the truth as I see it, I may as well go the full length of criticism and say that in regard to the scale of salaries she paid, she was not over-generous.

I have no complaint to make about her treatment of me, in this respect; for she paid the principals well enough. It is of the rank and file of her Ballet that I speak. There may be some justification for her attitude. She trained the girls and she taught them something that could not have been

acquired anywhere else in the world than in Pavlova's Ballet. It is a hallmark for a dancer to have
toured with Pavlova. A member of her Ballet always has a better chance of obtaining theatrical
work than any other competitor. I have heard
Pavlova say impatiently, "Why should I pay these
girls at all? They should pay me for the privilege
of belonging to my Company!"

There might be something to be said for this
point of view. Undoubtedly Pavlova, by her discipline of perfection, her insistence on detail, finish,
and endless exercising, practising and rehearsal,
improved the technique of any dancer who joined
her Ballet. It is also true that thousands of wealthy
amateurs, very likely, would have paid substan-
tially for the privilege of joining Pavlova's Company, if for only a short time. But the fact remains
that she did not accept premiums. She selected her
girls for their dancing only or for what she thought
she could make of them as dancers; and once they
had joined her Company and had been trained,
they were an integral part of the Company and
should have been remunerated in proportion as
the Company succeeded. It is all very well to talk
sentimentally of the Company being "one big

family", but a family should share good and bad alike. Bigger salaries would have been a more genuine token of her affection for her Company than all the small kindnesses with aspirin, birthday presents, and so on, by means of which Pavlova endeared herself to her girls.

I do not mean to convey that she was really mean about money. My impression is that she simply had no money sense whatever. She never carried money about on her person. I have seen her haggle about the price of a sixpenny object in a bazaar, and then authorize, later, a foolishly unnecessary expenditure of two hundred pounds. She would ask me, or others, to buy anything we happened to see which we thought she would like to have. In Aden, I remember how pleased she was when somebody bought her a number of ostrich-feather plumes, for her fan in "Rondino." Although she amassed a fortune, she did not dance for money and she did not *deliberately* exploit the people who travelled with her. She was a mystic of the dance. I have to keep insisting on this as the keynote of her character and career. Only the dance mattered. Many of the elements in her character which are most contradictory are resolved by this explanation.

Pavlova

Neither do I mean to convey by this criticism of her that the members of her Ballet were dissatisfied with their salaries. As an Englishman, with some conceptions of justice and the rights of working people, I was amazed by the apparently calm manner in which the members of her Company took what was given them without demur. There were plenty of dissensions and quarrels in the Company due to jealousies and rivalries as is inevitable among any considerable number of people blessed with the artistic temperament; but there was never any collective resentment against the management of the Company's affairs in respect to salaries and hours of work. By some extraordinary power of magnetism, Pavlova subdued the girls associated with her and seemed to be able to bend them to her own ambition. Great as she was in her art, she was therefore often unjust to those working with her.

She was a martinet of discipline — and that was all to the good: but she deliberately arranged the work of the other members of the Company in such a way as to form a background for her own work, irrespective of the talents and even the possibility of the genius of those others. Pavlova, for example, had a tendency to include tall girls in her

Ballet — so that she herself should appear even more "petite" than she was. This is good show-manship, no doubt; but it is a use of others which can only be made by the ruthless. When Pavlova was ruthless, she was merely expressing her own single-minded concentration on using the gift of God which was her own dancing.

Thus, if it was a wonderful experience for a ballet girl to be associated with Pavlova, it could also become a killing experience for those who stayed with her too long. Girls who have been dancing obscurely in Pavlova's Ballet have won recognition as stars almost immediately after leaving her. The liberation of their own personalities, after having been under her sway, was the explanation of their subsequent success.

I have digressed a little in order to show some of the cross-currents of emotion and ambition which were whirled in that torrent of energy called Pavlova. She had many things to think of. It was naturally a worry to be in charge of more than a score of young girls travelling in trains and ships, staying in hotels and strange towns — many of the girls away from home for the first time. Pavlova had to impress very strongly on the girls the necessity for

Pavlova

absolute propriety and moral sanity. The Pavlova Ballet had to be above reproach. But, also, there are certain practical disadvantages which may result from any intensification of the emotional life in people who are dedicated to work. . . .

Pavlova lived like a Spartan, if one can imagine an emotional Spartan. The members of her Company were expected to follow her example.

I have spoken of her inconsistency, and an amusing incident comes to mind. When we were at Singapore, I heard of an opportunity to do some angling in artificial ponds stocked with fish, about eighteen miles away. I mentioned the fact to Pavlova, who insisted on our setting out together early next morning before breakfast, although the boat was due to sail soon after midday. There were several ponds or tanks of fish, side by side, and a sum of money had to be paid to the management for each fish hooked. Pavlova fished in one tank and I in another near by. It so happened that I caught the first fish. Pavlova clapped her hands with excitement and insisted on transferring her rod and line to the tank where I was. "Perhaps I shall do better if I come to your tank!" she said.

Almost at once she got a "bite." She squealed

(110)

with alarm and then passed her rod to me, pirouetting by the waterside with glee. I wonder what would have been her fee for this charming little impromptu solo had she been commissioned to render it at a reception!

Just at the moment when she handed me her rod, a fish was hooked on my own line, so I landed both simultaneously! Pavlova was entranced and kept on fishing for more and more, until we almost missed the boat. She was very fond of eating fish. It was a favourite article of diet. One would have thought that she would have been more than pleased to take back such a fine haul to be prepared for her on board ship; the more so, as we had to pay for everything we hooked. But here comes her inconsistency — she insisted upon throwing all the fish back into the pond! She could not bear to see them gasping for air.

There was nothing she liked better, on the rare occasions when the Company had some leisure, than to organise a trip or a picnic to some local beauty spot. Thus in Java she planned an itinerary by motor car for the whole Company, not to take them to beauty spots recommended in the guide-books, but on a ramble along the roads selected by

herself. In Australia, too, there was a motor trip
to the famous Blue Mountains, and a picnic in the
Australian bush at which the traditional billy can
was boiled for tea. Pavlova on these little excursions
was a different person from the martinet of discipline and work in the theatre. She would romp and
run about, playing and shouting like any little
girl at a Sunday-school treat. Her nature was many-
sided, and one soon forgot all unpleasantness under
the influence of her irrepressible and girlish gaiety
at such times.

She had a queer sense of fun and enjoyed a practical joke. On one of our flying English tours, I
noticed, just as I was leaving an hotel, that one of
my gloves was missing. I had placed the gloves
with my hat and overcoat on a settee in the lounge
of the hotel about half an hour before the time set
for our departure, and as I only went to pick them
up at the last minute, I barely had time to make
indignant protests to the management about what
I supposed to be an ordinary theft, before leaving
to catch the train for the next town.

That same evening, shortly after my arrival at
the hotel in the next town, the postman brought
my missing glove with a piece of string tied around

it, and a label addressed from the hotel where my glove had been lost. I thought, at first, that the manager in response to my protests had found the glove and posted it on to me promptly, but the handwriting seemed familiar, and when I looked on the back of the label, I saw the words "From A. P." Having a few moments to spare before the departure from the hotel, she had taken my glove, labelled it and sent her maid out quickly to drop it in a post box.

To while away the tedium of long journeys in trains and on board ship, Pavlova enjoyed a card game called *Ramé*. She was anything but a stolid player and most emphatically expressed her delight or disappointment in winning or losing a trick. On one occasion she became positively furious, and with a kick sent the card table flying in a tornado of rage. People came rushing along the corridors of the train to see what on earth was the matter. . . .

Such occurrences were merely incidentals as we wandered everywhere, chained to the chariot of Anna Pavlova. She conquered more worlds than Alexander. She held sway over greater multitudes than Genghis Khan or Napoleon Bonaparte. She

Pavlova

was one of the few individuals in human history with a claim to genius — perhaps the only one — who was known in person wherever her reputation extended. Literary men, composers, artists, politicians are known by their works rather than in themselves. Even film stars, such as the well-loved Charles Chaplin, are known in their shadows rather than in themselves. But Anna Pavlova's genius was expressed by means of her personal presence. I cannot attempt to compute the hundreds of thousands of miles she has travelled and the multitudes of people into whose lives she has brought delight. Her power over people was a real thing. It was the power based on love and not on fear. It extended throughout every continent and transcended all barriers of race, religion and language. Surely what she has done is remarkable! It is thus that I think of Pavlova the tourist. The little incidents are scarcely worth chronicling.

I remember one which upset Pavlova extremely, because it was a manifestation of arrogance and adventitious power so utterly in contrast with everything she stood for. When we were at Milan, she had arranged for a sight-seeing trip to Como and back. In the train, one of the members of the

Company left his seat, which was quite near to that of Madame, and went to converse with his colleagues elsewhere in the coach. The train stopped at a wayside station and two Italians entered and occupied his vacant seat. Despite remonstrances, they would not give way when he returned. The guard was called. He merely had the member of our Company arrested at Milan for insults to Fascism! Our colleague was interrogated for several hours before being set free. It was impressed upon him that, as a foreigner, he should at once have given up his seat to an Italian when requested!

Pavlova felt personally affronted. To her the "incident" was one which should have been followed by at least formal international protests. That she, of all persons, should have been insulted as a "foreigner" at, of all places, Milan! Milan, the very birthplace of Classical Ballet — Milan, where the two people she respected more than any others on the earth, Cecchetti and Legnani, were that very evening to watch Pavlova dance!

Such an experience was rare. Usually Pavlova was paid great honour. When we were in Bombay, for example, there was a private performance by nautch girls one afternoon, with the Pavlova Com-

pany invited to be present in the capacity of audience, the entertainment being in honour of Pavlova and an expression of appreciation of the excellence of her own Indian dancing. It was an impressive spectacle. There were eight dancers and
an orchestra of five. Pavlova asked me if it would
be possible to transcribe the music for an European
orchestra. I had to express my doubts. The reed
instruments were of such a peculiar *timbre* that the
effect to European hearing was weird. In addition,
there was a singer who sang in quarter-tones and
eighth-tones, high pitched and nasal, producing
the effect of a whine; all of which would have been
lost if transferred to our European musical conceptions. As for the dancing itself, we could not follow
the finer points beyond realizing an effect of
tenderness. It was religious dancing and one would
have needed a knowledge of the symbolism to follow it. The dancing was with the arms, rather
than with the legs and feet. The costumes were of a
beautiful texture and sheen. Anna Pavlova was interested and perplexed. She recognized that the
dance was a beautiful expression of a religious emotion, and no doubt she learned much from it, for she
was never blind to anything original in her art.

Pavlova

Besides this, Eastern mysticism made a powerful appeal to her. She showed this in her ballet "Adjanta Frescoes" and also in "The Egyptian Mummy." I think she believed in reincarnation, and certainly she believed in, and practised, the self-transfiguring in mystic exaltation which characterizes Eastern religion.

I have mentioned previously the night which she spent alone in the desert before the Sphinx. No one will ever know what were her thoughts then. In the morning, when she came back to the hotel, all her Company were overcome with anxiety lest some mishap had befallen her; for she had insisted upon going out into the sand entirely alone. But when she came back there was a look of exaltation in her eyes and no sign of weariness. It may be said that she only did what any sentimental traveller could have done in thus electing to stay a night alone in the desert in the shadow of the pyramids. But I mention the occurrence here because it shows how Pavlova renewed her emotional forces from within by means of an esoteric process.

She had a similar mood of introspective mysticism when, at Agra, she visited the ruins of the old city and meditated at night in the temples.

Pavlova

Afterwards she described the Taj Mahal to me in what I thought were unusual words. She said that the Taj Mahal was a "cold blue marble dream." I learned later that she had gazed at the famous monument through an aperture in an old building many miles away, an aperture which revealed the distant Taj Mahal as a miniature set in a frame of stone. It was moonlight as she stood there, in a trance, and what is perhaps more astonishing to our conceptions of India, the night was bitterly cold.

I remember, too, her unnaturally sustained interest in the holy city of Benares and the embarrassing questions she kept on asking everybody about the Hindu faith. When in Calcutta we visited the burning ghat, we saw the body of an old man cremated with reverence by his son. Anna Pavlova thought this was very beautiful and expressed the wish that she too should be consumed by fire after her death. Several who were present remonstrated with her, saying that she had no need to talk of dying. But she said very sadly, "I shall die before any of you. I do not think I could possibly grow old and die slowly."

In Cairo she visited the Mosque. She was somewhat indignant because women occupied such an insignificant position in the Mohammedan estimation, this being with more particular reference to the view that women have no souls — a doctrine which Pavlova thought could easily be refuted. . . .

It was strange indeed to see her wearing the big over-slippers which are provided for visitors to the Mosque. Her habit in walking was to pick up the feet neatly at each step; but, swathed in slippers, she had to slide or almost waddle on the floor of the Mosque — a disconcerting sight to any one accustomed to seeing her usual daintiness of movement.

In stating that Pavlova was a mystic in religious matters, I do not mean that she had any acquaintance with the Eastern or any other religious philosophy as such. She was a remarkable *un*-literate woman. She seemed to have no interest in reading of any kind — with one exception, which is significant; she liked sometimes to read books of poems in any of the several languages with which she was familiar.

Neither had she any special knowledge of painting; but she indefatigably visited the art galleries wherever we went. She had no knowledge of art criticism or the history of art, but she was able intuitively to select good work from bad. Thus, at Rome, she preferred the small head of David by Michelangelo to the more famous full figure.

I remember that when we were in Australia she suddenly conceived the desire to learn how to paint! Borovansky, a member of the company, included among his achievements a technical ability in draughtsmanship and painting. Pavlova asked him to buy colours and canvases, and to teach her how to become a painter on the homeward journey! Borovansky duly purchased the materials but unhappily Madame became ill on board ship; otherwise, knowing her, I can be quite sure she would have applied herself to painting as she had already to sculpture; and it is almost equally certain that she would have painted, as she had modelled, little dancing subjects.

In various countries, as the Company travelled, enthusiastic admirers of Pavlova would follow her from town to town, in order to see as much of her dancing as possible before she left them, perhaps never to return. On one of our English tours, we were followed everywhere by a pleasant and uncommunicative old Scotchman, who must have been one of the most devoted *balletomanes* who ever lived. Despite the hackneyed jokes about Scotch closeness with money, he must have spent a small fortune in railway fares, let alone in box-office reservations, and I cannot but wonder at his pertinacity in following us, to see day after day the same performance — and moreover, to pay for it! Some members of the Company thought at first that he must be a private detective, but nobody appeared to be troubled with the necessary bad conscience to avoid him. Although he travelled on the same trains and stayed often at the same hotels, he did not try to become on intimate terms with anybody in the Company. Even when spoken to, he was not anxious to pursue conversations very far, least of all on the subject of ballet, to which all his actions proved he was blindly devoted. I do not think he even spoke to Pavlova, or made any effort to do anything other than watch her performances as though his life depended on that.

In Australia, too, the Company was followed for thousands of miles through all the States of that Continent by two girls who adored Madame. And when finally we left Perth in West Australia, they wept bitterly because they thought they might never see her dance again.

When travelling Pavlova liked to talk to everybody. She had a funny idiomatic expression to describe her predilection for social conversation. "I like to talk to everybody, *man to man*," she would say, and one understood perfectly what she meant. Considering her fame and the reverential awe in which she was held by so many people, she was quite unspoiled. No one has ever been able to describe Pavlova as a snob.

She was the strangest mixture of simplicity and stubborn determination. Thus I remember an occasion at Covent Garden market when a box of flowers she had bought in the early morning became mislaid. She insisted on finding out where the box had gone. The salesman offered her others "just as good", but she kept on saying, "Where are *my* flowers? Why do you think I come here so early in the morning if it is to be given the second-best?" The salesman finally confessed that her box had been sent in error on a motor van going to Oxford. Pavlova followed the van in her own car, overtook it at Reading and returned in triumph with her trophy to Ivy House at breakfast time!

Towards the end of her life she made a hobby of cinematography. She had two cameras of her own, one taking a full-size film, and one a smaller film. On our travels she would take films herself, and could hardly restrain her impatience until the films were developed and could be shown to the Company. Wherever we went she would make some arrangement for a private showing of her films. The results were sometimes unintentionally comic, out of focus, or badly "shot", but many of the films were quite good.

Then she had the idea of filming the Ballet. This was in Australia. She explained with enthusiasm to the Company that by means of her films they would be able to see themselves as the audience saw them. Accordingly the Company spent a week having three ballets filmed ("Don Quixote", "Invitation to the Waltz", "The Fairy Doll"). These were not film-studio performances, but ordinary performances in a theatre, with the camera in the dress circle. It was pointed out to Madame that the lighting was not of sufficient candle power. "Never mind," she said. "We'll get more lighting! Just let us try and see!"

Pavlova

A Hollywood film producer would have laughed at the arrangements for taking the film. The Company's electrician was the camera man. Remote in the dress circle, and without a megaphone, he had some difficulty in conveying to the dancers at what precise moments they were being "shot." He would start "shooting" before the dancers were ready. The result was that the films needed considerable "cutting" when they came to be shown, and there was many a laugh at the unconscious antics of the Ballet casually strolling about the stage. Before the week was up, a series of signals between the stage and the camera man had been arranged, and he had developed sufficiently stentorian tones to indicate when he was going to "shoot." One of the films was good. The incident illustrates Pavlova's enthusiasm for anything new, any available method of improving the Company's performance; but it is also an example of her enthusiasm for carrying out an idea of her own, regardless of drawbacks.

While she was at Hollywood, she became very friendly with Charles Chaplin. She has told me since that of all the theatrical artists she had met, she enjoyed his company most. Artistically, they

seem the strongest contrast conceivable, the one
known to the public as a tramp and a clown and a
grotesque comic figure; the other representing
ethereal grace and feminine charm and daintiness.
Yet these two great artists recognized the genius
of each other. Pavlova said to me that if Charles
Chaplin had been properly trained (*i.e.* at the Imperial School of Ballet) he would have become the
finest comedy dancer ever known! She thought
his miming was superb, and was amazed that any
one not "properly" trained could understand instinctively the importance of gesture and the sig-
nificance of mime.

At Hollywood she was also friendly with
Douglas Fairbanks and Mary Pickford. They
placed their magnificently equipped studio at her
disposal and with all the finest camera men and ap-
pliances an attempt was made to film her as she
danced. The result was not satisfactory, the reason
being that the lens of the camera was not fast
enough to catch her pirouettes, lighter than thistle-
down, and the vibrations of her finger tips. Since
then, such improvements have been made in film
cameras that it is a pity that she never had the opportunity of trying again, so that a permanent rec-

ord might have been left of her incomparable swiftness of limb.

I have mentioned previously the aviary which Pavlova had at Ivy House, stocked with birds from every quarter of the globe. As the Company journeyed, she would accumulate a greater and greater number of these pets. She carried them in cages built for their utmost comfort. As many as ten or a dozen of the cages went with us everywhere. Madame was more concerned for them than for her most valuable personal luggage. On trains her maids were distracted with worry, not knowing what to do with the birds. On liners she would make arrangements with the captain to have the cages placed in the most favorable part of the ship. When the wind changed its direction, or the ship altered its course, the "Zoo" (as the sailors invariably named the collection) had to be moved accordingly.

In spite of her care, many of the birds died. When Pavlova saw that one of her pets was ailing, she would prescribe and administer medicine. One morning early, on board ship, in the Indian Ocean, I saw a figure of inexpressible grief. It was Pavlova, disconsolate. As I came near, she called out to me, in tones of anguish, "Look what I have to show you to-day!" Lying in her palm were two birds, dead. No words of sympathy from me could have soothed the emotion she felt as she looked at the stiff little creatures of air, lying in her hands, their life of movement ended.

CHAPTER VI

Work

PAVLOVA knew only too well that the secret of perfection is in unremitting attention to detail and hard work. Many a time on our tours I have arrived at the theatre at nine-thirty in the morning, for a rehearsal called for ten o'clock, to find her already there, practising, doing her exercises on the stage. It was strange to see her, a solitary, delicate creature, pirouetting in the half-darkness of a vast empty stage, in a chill and deserted theatre. The rest of the Company would arrive, and begin "warming up" for the rehearsal. Woe betide any girl in the Company who neglected her practice exercises, or was not properly "warmed up" before a rehearsal of a performance! There would be no sympathy from Madame if an accident happened. "Why did you not loosen up properly?" she would say bitingly. "It serves you right. You will not be so lazy next time!"

Pavlova

An amusing incident occured once in Australia when Pavlova was practising in the early morning by herself. A stage carpenter told her to get out of his way and go to practise somewhere else! With her perfect understanding of theatrical niceties, Pavlova was not affronted. She went meekly away as directed. "The man was quite within his rights," she commented afterwards, and that settled the matter, as far as she was concerned.

She was not always so meek. During rehearsals of dances in which she did not appear personally, Madame would keep warm by exercising at the side of the stage, using for a bar anything that came to hand, but watching the rehearsal keenly all the time. At unexpected moments, often when everybody else concerned thought that things were going very well, her voice would ring out sharply, "Do that again!" or "That is all wrong!" I have known her insist on rehearsing for an hour and a half a movement which takes only *ten seconds* in execution.

Sometimes she was at variance with her balletmaster — or even her musical director! As regards ballet, she was always ready to listen to Fokine or Clustine, but I recall one stormy scene in which

Pianowsky resigned because of a difference of opinion from Madame. There were occasions, when, out of sheer devilment, it seemed, she absolutely would not give way, though she knew herself to be in the wrong. Once on tour in Germany her partner Novikoff ventured to suggest that Madame was exerting herself unnecessarily in a certain movement. She knew at once that he was right, but she would not alter her method. She continued to do the movement in her own way. She gave the *most difficult rendering* of the step. But this, too, was characteristic of her. She was obstinate and wrong often enough; but she never spared herself.

She was thorough, unbelievably thorough, in the preparation and rehearsals of her ballets. When audiences applauded the apparent spontaneity of the Ballet's movements, very few in the front of the house could have imagined the discipline and endless routine of rehearsals by which that perfection had been attained. Every movement, every gesture, every position on the stage had to be exactly as Madame wanted it, and she would keep the Company at rehearsal until her effect was achieved. Even the lighting effects she did not leave to the good intentions of the electrician. Pavlova herself would go out into the auditorium during rehearsals and make the most careful notes and comments on the lighting of the stage in each theatre we visited.

I remember one occasion on which she rebuked members of the Company who were dancing in Hungarian costume because they did not have a sufficient number of necklaces! Every ribbon, every detail of costume and make-up, had to be as perfect as the execution of the steps and movements in the dance itself.

She was likely to become excited when things were going wrong. She expected people to understand her when often, in her excitement, she could not explain what it was that she wanted. In Russian, French, German, or English, she would remonstrate and attempt to explain, tossing her head, stamping her feet with impatience. For example, if she wanted certain alterations in the music, she could not always convey to me what she wanted because she did not know the technical expressions necessary. On such occasions she would work herself up from a slight impatience to a condition of raging frenzy. The storm would pass, as storms do;

but she was not the only one who could become excited. I do not mind admitting that once, in Buenos Aires, I lost my temper and gave as good an exhibition of Russian "temperament" as could be expected from a naturally phlegmatic Staffordshire man. I remembered my football days, and kicked a musical score from the orchestra on to the stage!

If she could become excited when things were going wrong, she could become equally excited when something pleased her. When a member of the ballet did a step particularly well, Madame would jump about like a little girl, clapping her hands with merriment and delight, and excitedly calling out *"Harascho!"* (good!)

She was sensitive to anything that could affect her attitude towards her work. Often I have seen her at rehearsal, not in the usual practice dress, but in a ballet skirt with bodice and a little shawl. It would have been easier to wear a practice dress, but she never took the easier way. We may surmise that the fluffiness of the ballet skirt gave her something, a quality of lightness, a feeling of elation, which made even her practice or rehearsal an expression of an art and not a dull discipline.

PAVLOVA IN THE DRAGON-FLY DANCE

Pavlova

To be praised by Madame at rehearsal was a prize well worth the winning, but in her endeavor for perfection in everything, she was not always just in her censure. She was inclined to be whimsical in exerting her authority. I have known her, for example, say to a girl in her Ballet, "What a terrible make-up! For goodness' sake alter it at once!" Not knowing exactly what Madame wanted, the girl would retire to the dressing room and reappear in due course with exactly the same make-up as before. Whereupon Madame would say, "There! You see! What a vast improvement!" Yet Anna Pavlova won the genuine esteem and respect of those working with her, quite apart from the respect due to her unquestionably supreme art and the authority of her world-famous name.

Rehearsals were usually called for ten o'clock in the morning. When we arrived at a big town where a season of several weeks was to be given, there was much to be done, and quickly, on the first day of our arrival. The "call" to the orchestra for the first rehearsal had already been given in advance, and the ballet-master would let the Company know while we were still travelling, the day before our arrival. There was a great bustle and activity in the theatre as the time arrived for the rehearsal to begin.

Scene shifters, stage hands, electricians, would be going about their jobs, hammering and clattering. The orchestra (sometimes consisting of from sixty to seventy players) would be settling into their seats, unpacking their instruments, tuning up, and so on. No scenery would yet be in position on the stage, and on the expanse thus revealed figures in overalls would be hurrying about, while groups of the dancers would be "warming up", practising steps and doing exercises. The dim auditorium would be deserted, rows of seats draped with dust sheets giving the effect of the ghost of an audience at a spectacle without meaning. Then Madame would give a sign, the ballet-master would take up his position on a chair in the centre, and the rehearsal would begin.

There was usually a preliminary rehearsal of the ballet and the orchestra separately, before the joint rehearsal. The safety curtain would be let down, a piano on the stage providing the music for rehearsing the Ballet, whilst I went over the music separately with the orchestra. Despite all precautions, there was often something overlooked,

no piano on the stage, broken music stands not re-
paired — dozens of annoying, if trivial, delays in
beginning.

Sometimes the safety curtain would not be
sound-proof, and the Ballet would be disturbed
by the orchestra playing a different piece from that
which they were dancing. Madame would send
word to me, asking if the orchestra could rehearse
more quietly, a request difficult to accede to. On
these occasions the Ballet sometimes rehearsed in
the foyer, if large enough for that purpose.

At last the safety curtain would be raised and
the Ballet would rehearse, with orchestra, to the
additional accompaniment of hammering by stage
carpenters, and the bawling of instructions to the
flies and "limes" overhead. The ballet-master
would clap his hands as a signal to the Company
for attention, and I would begin on the first number to be rehearsed. There would be frequent
halts. Sometimes the actual tempo of a dance would
have to be altered to suit the size of a stage, smaller
stages making certain evolutions unduly difficult.
Each player in the orchestra and each dancer in
the Ballet would have to note and remember such
an alteration in the tempo.

Pavlova

Some of the stages had an unduly big "rake" (or slope) which, from the dancers' point of view, was not only uncomfortable, but in some evolutions difficult and dangerous. Some stages were of especially hard wood, which was most painful for dancing on the *point*. To adjust the ballet and the music to these peculiarities of the stage often necessitated a considerable delay, while the scenery was set, to see just what was required. During all this time, Anna Pavlova would never stop exercising, using for a bar the proscenium wing, a rung of a ladder fixed to the wall, or even a dress basket.

In ballets or numbers in which she did not appear, she liked to come down into the stalls. Frequently, she would lean over the orchestra rail by my side, while commenting on points of the rehearsal and chatting to me. As she watched, she would begin her perpetual exercising, with a hand on the orchestra rail. "What a waste of a good bar!" she would say. "Why do they not have it on the stage?" Her restless eyes would be intently watching what was happening. Sometimes she would stop the rehearsal and have the whole orchestra raised (by means of planks) so that the music could be heard better by the dancers, if the front of the stage projected over the pit. Sometimes she absolutely dominated the rehearsal and nothing pleased her. At other times, she was silent, noting everything, and yet leaving matters to her ballet-master.

When she was dancing to an instrumental solo, there was always an anxious moment for me at the first rehearsal. I had to do with all sorts and conditions of performers, good, bad and wretched. Pavlova could tell after a few bars whether the instrumentalist's interpretation suited her. When the performer was not suiting her, she would stop her dance and come forward to the footlights. She would bend forward, stooping over towards the instrumentalist, with her hands clasped together between her knees. Then, in her staccato voice, she would ask him to play the music as he felt it. "All right now," she would say, "you play for me. I dance for you. Cannot you feel the music as I dance? You play the music for me as you feel it." These tactics were not always successful. Not even Pavlova's charm could effect the magic of trans-forming a bad player into a good one at a moment's notice.

She was delighted if her soloist was good and her dance brilliantly played. On these occasions she would say, "Excellent! What can I say more? Why cannot it always happen so?" After the performance she would remember to send word to me to convey her thanks and appreciation to the instrumental soloist. I have even seen her throw a flower from her bouquet to the 'cellist after "The Swan"; but this was very rare indeed. Pablo Casals once played this solo for her.

There were times when it was impossible to rehearse the orchestra sufficiently in the music as she wanted it played. In some theatres the orchestra was composed of such poor material, musically speaking, that in the time available for rehearsal, I could see inevitable difficulties ahead. In the South of Germany (of all places) I have had to conduct performances with a grand piano on a platform immediately in front of me, so that in the event of the music breaking down, I should be able to stop the orchestra and play the rest of the music on the piano. A strange tradition still persists in parts of Germany that the orchestra is a military organization. Visiting conductors are warned by theatre managements not to be overpolite towards the instrumentalists — never to address them as "gentlemen" and above all never to say "please."

The worst orchestra in all my experience was in Bombay where, after hours of rehearsal, the only result I could achieve can best be described as a diabolical cacophony.

Pavlova danced in all kinds of theatres, and when the Company arrived at each new town, one of the first anxieties of Madame was to inspect the stage surface minutely. She never danced on a cloth unless the board surface was absolutely hopeless. Linoleum-covered stages were particularly bad for dancing. Pavlova hated linoleum. She said it made her feet *burn* and that she would rather dance on red-hot bricks!

After her inspection it was generally necessary to hammer and plane the bumpy or uneven parts of the stage surface. An irregularity, or a notch, or hole, would have been disastrous, resulting in a twisted ankle or knee, had she caught her toe in it. She took trouble to test every part of the stage, feeling doubtful parts with the sole of her shoe. Sometimes a new plank had to be let in. If, despite these precautions, Pavlova subsequently found a weak spot in the floor, she would make a point of dancing away from that place, no easy achievement when one considers the complicated and rapid evolutions of her dances.

The special preparations before the performances were interesting. The stage was first swept carefully, then watered to a precise degree, as it was important not to have wet and slippery patches. Next, the stage was sprinkled with powdered resin. (The dancers also used resin trays in the wings to give their shoes the best possible foothold.)

On one occasion, an obliging management prepared a pleasant "surprise" for Pavlova, intending to do her the greatest possible honour. Seeing her anxiety in scrutinizing the surface for irregularities, they engaged a small army of polishers, who worked furiously with furniture polish in the late afternoon after the rehearsal. When Madame arrived at the theatre, the management led her to inspect their work. The stage was shining and smoother than glass! Madame almost collapsed with astonishment and laughed hysterically in the faces of her well-intentioned benefactors. Without a moment's delay, another miniature army had to be got together to sandpaper every square inch of the floor and to remove all its lustrous polish. Even then, the performance was twenty minutes late in starting.

The memory work of a big repertoire of ballets and divertissements was terrific, and cannot solely be explained by the adage "Practice makes perfect." Yet I have known Pavlova have astonishing lapses of memory. She has remonstrated with me at rehearsals about details of the music, saying (for example), "Surely there is no *gama* there!" This, despite the fact that I would have the score before me, to settle the argument, and further despite the fact that she had heard the same music played, and had danced to it, hundreds or even thousands of times!

Her opinions on the way music should be played were enough to drive a conductor to distraction. It was impossible to explain to Pavlova that the composer was the best judge of the tempo in which his work should be taken. Pavlova wanted it faster here; slower there; phrases cut out; phrases inserted, sustained notes held absurdly. Instead of dancing to the music, she wanted the music to be played in time to her. The tempo had even to be altered if the stage was small; but chiefly if Pavlova wanted to have it altered for no reason at all.

Pavlova

She would listen attentively enough when I played over a new work to her. As she listened, she would be mentally, and sometimes physically, working out steps. Then I would have to be prepared for an interruption. She would say, "That passage should be much slower", or "I should like that twice as fast." What use then to argue with her: "It is all very well to make the tempo elastic, but you cannot possibly turn an *adagio* into an *allegro!*"

The explanation of her apparent crassness in regard to the interpretation of music is that she could not play any kind of musical instrument whatsoever. I have often regretted that Pavlova was not an executant on some musical instrument. Her body was the only musical instrument she knew how to play.

In orchestral pieces she could not understand, for example, that a wood-wind passage cannot be played on the trumpet. She would say, "That would be better if you had the trumpet bring it out more loudly!"

I found it absolutely impossible to explain to her why this could not be done. I remember once at a rehearsal of the "Egyptian Mummy", the score of Arensky's Valse was mislaid — all except the first oboe part. Pavlova was not dismayed. She said, "Never mind. We can rehearse with the piano, using the oboe part!" She was incredulously indignant when I pointed out (I speak now from memory) that the oboe part began with twenty bars' rest!

This criticism of her apparent musical unintelligence is one which I make with the caution that it is not intended to belittle her artistry as a dancer. Her musical perception, if we consider her interpretation of a *complete musical theme,* was uncannily good. But in regard to detail, her musical knowledge was by no means equal to her musical sensibility.

Because she preferred romantic music — any modern harmonies or dissonant chords disturbed her — she was precluded by what was almost a physical shortcoming from the interpretation of modern masterpieces. But even in the music she preferred, her arbitrary breaking up of the phrases spoiled the melody and rhythm by making it choppy and disconnected.

To work with her was like being a disciple of a Messiah. She regarded herself as infallible. She was structurally incapable of understanding that other people could not see things from her point of view — or, indeed, that there could possibly be any other point of view than her own. She would become almost hysterical when contradicted and would suffer from depression afterwards. In one of these moods, her maid once said to her, "Sometimes, Madame, there are two opinions, and both are right. Other people are entitled to have a different opinion from yours, and still not be wrong!" Pavlova was astonished at this simple dictum and pondered over it for several days. Then, with the air of one experiencing a great revelation, she said, "You are right. I have never realized it before. It is quite possible that even when people contradict me they are not deliberately trying to annoy me. I will try to remember this in future, but it will be difficult."

But, as a rule, it was no use remonstrating with her. She would lose her temper and become an inferno of incoherence, abuse, insult and imprecation.

She was impatient enough with anybody who could not learn a dance immediately, yet she was oh, so slow herself to learn anything new! The music had to be repeated *ad nauseam* before she could remember the steps. Then to make matters worse, after she had learned the dance perfectly, she would proceed to introduce her own variations in tempo. A conductor would develop eye strain, heart strain, and nerve strain, trying to synchronize the orchestra with her frantic feet. She was aware of this difficulty, of course, and took an impish pleasure, sometimes, in trying to make a fool of the conductor by suddenly jumping out of her position after giving preliminary indications that she was going to hold it for some moments.

No dance was ever the same twice. If she felt well, her dancing was uncontrollable — even by herself. She was a being possessed. If she felt at cross-purposes with the world and herself, she was just as likely to be sulky in a dance as not. The audience, of course, would not detect her sulking. But for the man trying to follow her musically, it was obvious enough.

Yet she was always likely to lose her temper with the other dancers, or with one of them, if *their* dances did not happen to synchronize exactly with the music and the movement of the rest of the ballet. Her favourite term of abuse was to call one of the girls in such circumstances a "cow" — than which there could scarcely be any epithet more injurious to a ballet dancer; who, theoretically, has little resemblance to that useful animal. But the Company understood Pavlova and could put up with her fits of temper and her abusiveness, because they knew that in a few moments she was just as likely to become excessively gracious and affectionate. The Company knew, too, the terrible strain under which she lived and worked.

With the exception of a few ballets, the music to which Pavlova danced was commonplace enough. She seemed to wish to avoid the really great works of such composers as Beethoven, Brahms, Bach, and Mozart, probably because she was steeped in the traditional ballet and had a subconscious leaning towards the more obvious music. Thus the rhythms which she preferred were of an elementary kind. It was actually very difficult for her, in a composition in which there were two contrasting rhythms, to concentrate sufficiently on one without being distracted by the other. This merely shows that she was a dancer first, and that music was, for her, only a secondary consideration.

In learning a new dance, she practised it by the spacing of the music, counting the bars singly and

PAVLOVA AND ALEXANDER VOLININE

not as the music required, by taking a phrase in its
entirety. The result was musically incongruous
when frequently she would begin a new movement
in the middle of a phrase. Such a bizarre punctua-
tion of the music gave it a completely different
meaning from that which the composer intended.

After rehearsals, often when the rest of the
Company would be enjoying a relaxation, Pavlova would have to remain in the theatre for one
reason or another. In almost every town we visited
she had to go through the ordeal of being photographed for the Press or by "artistic" studios who
wished to enjoy the kudos of showing her pictures,
as taken by them, in their windows. It was a matter of routine for Pavlova to arrange a specific time
for being photographed. She would have to make
herself up for the purpose — all of which was unnecessarily tiring for her. Then, when everything
was ready, she would pose before the battery of
cameras and the shutters would click — not always
catching her to the best advantage. It was usual for
photographs so taken to be submitted to her for
approval before publication. She had a curious
facility for retouching photographs with a pencil,
blacking out harsh light effects and contours. Pro-

fessional photographers were amazed at her gifts in this direction and would express sincere admiration for her understanding of the pictorial quality in a photograph.

Again, there was the ordeal of watching the dances of beginners. When she was at the height of her fame and a household name throughout the world, she was never too self-important or too busy to see and criticize the worth of aspirants to dancing fame. Pavlova was never sarcastic at these "auditions", though it is a fact that she simply could not understand why a girl could not do certain steps. She would put the girls at their ease and in this way she has given encouragement to thousands of young dancers in every part of the world. This reminds me of an amusing incident at Covent Garden which illustrates how the very name and fame of Pavlova frightened young aspirants (unnecessarily). Madame asked a girl to do a step, and she replied, "You must excuse me, Madame, I cannot hear you; *I am short-sighted!*"

Sometimes she attended these auditions between a matinée and an evening performance, when, by all the rules of common sense, she should have been resting. She never let the girls know that their performances bored her, though afterwards she might remark to some one in the Company, "How hopeless people are! How blind and vain and fatuous!"

I could never quite understand why she allowed herself to be imposed upon in this way. She knew quite well, or ought to have known after so many years of it, that the pupils of provincial and colonial dancing academies, however ambitious and well-intentioned, were not likely to be able to do anything in the way of dancing to interest Madame Pavlova. Yet these inane auditions took place as of right almost everywhere we went. I cannot imagine that Pavlova deceived herself to the extent of believing that one day she might "discover" a genius. Genius discovers itself, as Pavlova ought to have known. The Company, who loved Pavlova, for all her faults, were exceedingly resentful of the demands made upon her time and energy by her attendance at the exhibitions of these amateurs. It was no doubt irritating to girls in her Ballet to hear her murmuring sweet praise of amateurish work — when their own work, incomparably better, had perhaps only just previously received Madame's sarcastic censure. Yet Pavlova has given encouragement to several young dancers who subsequently made names for themselves in the theatre. If she never discovered a genius equal to her own, she has by her kindly interest provided the necessary stimulus to talent on more than one occasion.

She used to help people in strange ways. In South America the Company was set to work hard at the rehearsals of a new "Redskin" ballet. For a long time it was not understood why the ballet was never produced after so much time had been expended on it. The scenery had been sketched and the dresses had been designed. It appeared, afterwards, that Pavlova, in order to help the creator of this ballet — a Russian refugee — had commissioned him to rehearse the ballet for production. Some of the work was particularly hard on the *corps-de-ballet,* but this fact did not occur to Pavlova. In order to recompense the refugee for his work, she gave him a substantial cheque. It will be noted that she did not spare herself the hard work of rehearsal on this occasion.

It was thus by precept and by example that Pavlova inspired the whole of her Ballet with the principle that as far as dancing is concerned it is impossible to work too much. She would impress upon them, by precept and example, that no one's technique is so perfect that it cannot be improved by hard work and relentless practising. Because she worked like a slave herself, it was impossible for any one to grumble behind her back that she was a slave driver. If the girls practised only three-quarters of the time that Pavlova herself practised they would have been giving more time each day to their work than any other dancers in the world. There were compensations in this life of devotion which Pavlova compelled from those who were associated with her — the satisfaction that everything humanly possible was being done to achieve perfection; the satisfaction of a performance so finished in its details as to give pleasure to the dancer herself; for the audience would never realize subtleties of technique and difficulties of execution, so effortless did they become in the Pavlova Ballet as the result of perpetual drilling.

Besides, if any one in the Company did not like Pavlova's methods, he or she could leave and go somewhere else, where life would be less strenuous. Because this grand principle exists, weaklings were excluded from the Company of Anna Pavlova.

CHAPTER VII

The Dancer

BEFORE the curtain went up, Pavlova was on the stage with the whole Company, "warming up" with practice steps for an hour. Then she would take delight in watching her girls practising and inventing new steps of their own, and would encourage them and criticize and help. The greatest dancer of our age was not above learning something new from a young girl of the Ballet. She was alert for these new and spontaneous developments in her art, and would incorporate the steps so acquired in her subsequent ballets.

As she stood in the wings waiting to go on the stage, Pavlova could *sense* the feeling of the waiting audience. She would say: "It's a good audience to-night", or "It's a hard audience", and her intuition was never wrong. She understood that, from the moment she came into the lights, it was herself *versus* the audience — her volatile dy-

namic power *versus* the dullness and lethargia behind those rows of dim faces peering at her. She
knew how to cross that most formidable of all barriers, the footlights. She knew how to fill all a
theatre with her personality, this frail little thing
— how to take an audience by the scruff of its
neck and shake it into animation and then wheedle
it into delight. Let them be ever so solidly anchored
to earth, those shirt fronts covering substantial din-
ners, Pavlova could make them flutter with the
breath of the spirit, and she knew it.

She seemed to nerve herself for an effort as she
listened for the music to accompany her entry. At
the last moment she would draw herself up to her
full height, take a quick deep breath, moisten her
lips, at the same time smoothing her waist inwards
with the palms of her hands on her hips. This gesture was involuntary and she never failed to make
it. It was as though she was gathering herself together spiritually; it was like a magic ritual to
banish Pavlova of the flesh and evoke Pavlova the
spirit of dance. The gesture always ended with a
quick backward movement of the right hand, as
though she were pushing at something unseen behind her, an invisible force which gave her momen-

tum for the whole of her dance. Then she would glide on to the stage into view of the audience, and from that second until she retired she was an embodied ecstasy.

It may seem remarkable that such a great star as Anna Pavlova never really became accustomed to presenting herself to an audience, yet such was the fact. She was nervous before she made her first appearance, at any performance. As *the* Pavlova she managed to conceal this stage fright and to show some appearance of being calm and collected; but to those who knew her intimately it was evident that she had always to make an effort to overcome her nerves.

In an emergency she was coolness itself. Her stage sense and her showmanship were amongst her greatest assets. She allowed no mishap to affect a solo number or an ensemble during the performance of a ballet. Frequently, from the wings, she would take charge of a situation if things were going wrong and tell the other dancers what to do.

In her dances she was an erratic performer. She would become entranced with her own bodily rhythm, would lose herself in the dance, and quite frequently would hold a pose longer than the music to which she was dancing warranted. This was another embarrassment to the conductor of the orchestra. I have had to hold an orchestra in leash, watchful for the moment when she would move from a pose that no other dancer on earth could have held for a fraction of the time. She would sometimes hold her position "on the point" with such perfect balance and for such a length of time that one gasped with amazement that such a thing should be physically possible.

A dancer is an interpreter and holds the same relation to the choreographer as does the executant to the composer. A violinist or a pianist, for instance, having studied a certain composition, and having been shown how to do it by a great teacher, might actually play the composition perfectly — but it would mean nothing to the listener. The intricacies of technique might be perfect. Yet for all the brilliance, the hearer might be left unmoved. It is the same with dancers. Unless there is in the soul of the dancer that something of personality which is allied to technique so that one feels an emotion from the dance — then it is purely a matter of technique and nothing else. Many dancers could dance — and have danced — the rôles that Pavlova has played, but none of them have been able to give that extra something, call it personality, artistry, feeling, or what you will, that she did.

Pavlova in the dance was an independent thinker. Quite apart from the personality that was peculiarly Pavlova's, one of the secrets of her success was her untiring personal application to detail. Having had the general scheme of the dance given to her, she would practise the minor details so assiduously, linking up one to the other by gradual degrees, that in the end so much did the movements become second nature to her that she was able to forget all about them and technically she had to think of the dance no more. She was then able to give *her* meaning to the dance, to portray to the onlooker what *she* felt, and that is why it was not surprising that often Pavlova would interpret the same dance in a different manner.

The result, however charming to audiences, was a nightmare to her Musical Director. For example, in her divertissement danced to Drigo's "Serenade", she was incorrigible. This is a simple *pas de deux* between Harlequin and Pierrette which displayed, as well as any other dance she did, her wonderful arabesque, balancing on the *point,* and pirouettes. Pavlova was never satisfied with the music. She seemed unable to comprehend the fact that a small orchestra in Singapore or Bundaberg cannot be expected, after one rehearsal, to produce the same quality of tone as the grand orchestra of the Mariansky Theatre, where she had danced this "Serenade" as a girl. However, I would do my best when she grumbled. Once, after a performance which had displeased her, I decided to settle the argument then and there. I went over the music with her on a piano, phrase by phrase, and insisted that she should indicate exactly what she wanted. Then I recorded the metronomic marking of the approved tempi! Next day, I rehearsed the piece with the orchestra for more than three quarters of an hour, until it was exactly what she had approved. She was present at this rehearsal and after the orchestra had twice played the number, she rehearsed the dance on the stage. All had gone smoothly. Pavlova was pleased, and I was pleased. "Now," she said, "for to-night we will keep it as it is." At the performance that evening, I conducted it as we had together rehearsed it.

She was furious. Her mood had changed, she

said. What on earth did I mean by playing her dance in that tempo? She had to dance just as she felt, and so on. I sighed, and said, "Very well then! Let us be simple people again and for once play the thing as Drigo wants it played." At the end of our exchange of ideas Pavlova admitted that musically I was justified; but in spite of all, she claimed the right to dance as she felt. This, I regret to say, was always a bone of contention, and many battles royal did we have regarding composers' ideas and tempi.

Her moments of elation would be peculiarly reflected in one of her variations. One could always see when she was enjoying herself, and in these moods she was uncanny. She would forget all about technique, about herself, about her audience, and hold positions for an ecstatic eternity. At these moments she would seem to float and not to touch the stage at all. It seemed as if she were defying the laws of gravitation and doing something preposterously marvellous. One knew when these occasions would come round. One could tell by the twinkle of merriment in her eyes.

When her dance was finished, Pavlova would quickly take a sip of water and dab herself with a

Pavlova

powder puff taken from a tray held by her maid
waiting in the wings, while the applause from the
auditorium would be swelling tumultuously. Pavlova *never failed* to please an audience. In every
part of the world it was the same. I have never
known an audience that was not enthused by her
dance.

She loved applause, but she did not dance in
order to win applause. She would have been
amazed indeed if an audience had not applauded
her, yet at every performance she was naïvely
pleased because her work had given pleasure. Her
eyes would sparkle like any schoolgirl's at an
amateur concert, when, after one of her wonderful
dances, the audience would begin acclamations.
In many ways such as this she was amazingly simple in character. It was not the usual theatrical
vanity which made her take such a delight in applause; it was a real feeling of joy because she had
done something to please those strange heavy people beyond the footlights. She never came to take
applause for granted. She earned it anew, as a
phenomenal thing, at each performance.

At precisely the right moment she would make
her quick ritual gesture in the wings, then emerge

(159)

to "take her call." She was an adept at taking a call. Every gesture, every movement, was perfect. Frequently her calls for "The Swan" lasted longer than the dance itself. I have never known Pavlova give an encore to "The Swan." Artistically, to have done so would have been as wrong as could be. With her insight into the psychology of an audience she knew this. She refused to spoil an effect, which depends upon climax, by repeating the effect, however much the audience might beg her to do so.

After the finale came the bouquets. Pavlova's winsomeness was never better expressed than when the flowers were handed up to her and she would share them with the girls of the Ballet, in view of the audience, to express her pleasure at the dancing of the other members of her Company. She never allowed anything but flowers to be handed across the footlights. The audience caught their last glimpse of her clasping a bouquet of flowers.

She could not relax until after she had received the compliments and respects of visitors in her dressing room. At midnight she had supper, her principal meal of the day. She ate, as she lived, temperamentally. When she took food, she ate

THE END OF THE SWAN DANCE

heartily; at other times she merely pecked, like a bird. She drank with moderation, nothing more than a glass of wine occasionally. Her life was austere in all its personal phases, apart from work. She tried to avoid after-theatre parties and festivities. She had to keep herself physically fit and she knew it. She gave so much of herself to her work that she needed all her strength for that.

And when I say work, I mean it. Pavlova worked, more often than not, *for fifteen hours a day at least,* or about twice the number of hours universally sanctioned as a fair thing. Lest this statement should appear incredible, particularly to stage-struck young ladies who think that theatrical people live in the lap of luxury and ease, I give some details of Pavlova's actual working schedules.

She was working (that is "on the go", not able to relax) for approximately five hours at each performance. From the point of view of the audience, an evening performance lasted from somewhere about eight o'clock until shortly after eleven — three hours. Pavlova was in the theatre from seven o'clock until midnight — five hours.

Before the performance began, she would be on the stage for an hour, warming up with practice steps or conducting a last-minute rehearsal until only a few moments before the curtain went up.

A typical Pavlova programme was divided into three parts of about fifty minutes each, with intervals between. The first two parts were complete and separate ballets, the third part of the programme being a series of about seven dance numbers or divertissements. Let us compute the amount of actual work done by her at a typical performance. Let us suppose the programme be as follows:

Part I. Ballet in One Act.

AMARILLA........................*Glazounow-Drigo*

PAVLOVA, in the title rôle, as the gypsy maiden, has several sustained passages of mime, three solo dances — an adagio, a valse, and a galop — and a variation in the ensemble.

Part II. Ballet in One Act.

SNOWFLAKES ....*Tschaikowski*

PAVLOVA, in the principal rôle, dances a big adagio *(pas de deux),* a variation in the ensemble, and the coda.

Pavlova

Part III. Divertissements.

1. Hungarian Rhapsody......................*Liszt*
   (The Company)
2. Rondino.....................*Beethoven-Kreisler*
   (Pas Seul — ANNA PAVLOVA)
3. Anitra's Dance...........................*Grieg*
   (Pas Seul)
4. Menuet............................*Paderewski*
   (Pas de deux)
5. Pizzicato................................*Drigo*
   (Pas de cinq)
6. Spanish Dance...........................*Bizet*
   (Pas seul)
7. Russian Dance.........*Rubenstein-Tschaikowski*
   (Ensemble, with three variations by PAVLOVA)

A glance at this average programme shows several interesting things; for one, her conventional taste in music, which is not the point here and is referred to elsewhere. I have made this programme up as a fair sample of what she presented to an audience at any one performance. The programmes were arranged on this model in all the permutations of twenty or more ballets and at least one hundred divertissements which the Company included in its repertoire.

Pavlova

It will be noticed that in my specimen programme, Pavlova dances eleven distinct and separate numbers and has four changes of costume and make-up. This is what I mean by saying that during the performance she worked hard. She had, on an average, from ten to a dozen dances personally and from four to six changes of costume and make-up.

In each of her ballets, of course, her work was sustained throughout and included long passages of mime, which in her work was more than mime — it was intense emotional acting. In ballets such as "Giselle" and "Amarilla" she gave herself unrestrainedly to the tragedy of the theme and would be utterly exhausted when the final curtain came down. In ballets such as "The Fairy Doll" and "La Fille Mal Gardée" she had pure comedy parts and bubbled over with gaiety, keeping the audiences in a continual state of merriment.

In Part III of the programme, it will be noticed that Pavlova's numbers were Number 2 and Number 7. This was invariably so. Number 2 was a solo or a dance with partner. It was here that she danced "The Swan", "Gavotte Pavlova", "Valse Caprice", "Californian Poppy", "Les Papillons", etc. Number 7 was a big divertissement, almost a short ballet, or a suite of dances, such as "The Mexican Dances", Poncinelli's "Dance of the Hours", "Pas Hongrois", and "The Polish Mazurka", etc., in which Pavlova had two or three variations, either solo or with partner.

After the performance she would be confined to her dressing room to receive visitors for about half an hour before she could change and remove her make-up and leave the theatre. When there was a matinée, which was at least twice a week and very often more, she was in the theatre from about half past one, without a moment's proper relaxation, until midnight. Often between the matinée and the evening performance there would be the "auditions" already mentioned — otherwise they would take place in the afternoon.

Rehearsals took place in the morning at ten o'clock and lasted at least two hours. In the early morning, before rehearsals, Pavlova practised by herself. I am making quite a conservative estimate when I say that this paragon of a dancer worked — and worked intensely hard — for fifteen hours each day. She took eight hours' sleep and one hour's leisure.

Pavlova

Enough of the quantity of work she did — it is the quality that mattered! I cannot describe the quality of her dancing. Famous literary men and critics in every country have tried, but without success. Poets have tried to praise her — a blind poet, who once went to her performance, with his sixth sense got nearer to understanding Pavlova's magic than those of us who have merely watched her as she danced.

A friend of mine, an author, went to see her at Covent Garden, and he said to me afterwards, "I may be laughed at, and called old-fashioned and all that, but when she floated on to the stage in 'The Swan', I felt a cold shiver in my spine and realized at once that I too would soon have to die, and I wondered if death was really as beautiful as that. . . ."

Words cannot describe Pavlova's dancing, for words are too concrete and rigid. Her dancing was a distillation of the soul — like the fragrance of a flower which can be recognized but not described, or like the scintillating light of a gem.

If in this book I have set down many incidents which may seem trivial, it is only that I have despaired of describing Pavlova the genius except through a number of little facets which the reader may recognize as belonging to the gem, though not explaining the gem's inner brilliance.

To use her own words "Some people *shine* through more than others." Pavlova's inner light was as lovely as a diamond's light, dazzling the eyes, but like nothing other than itself; indescribable, incomparable, scintillating with its own elusive quality. Find words to describe a diamond's light to a person who has not seen a diamond, or find words to describe the perfume of a flower; you may then be a poet great enough to describe Pavlova's dancing to some one who has not seen Pavlova.

But although she had the gemlike hardness and brilliance of a diamond, she was not a stone; she was *alive* with dynamic energy; she radiated a living light-quality. What she gave out was not merely refracted; it was alive, renewed from her human forces. And her dancing was more real and tangible and alive than the perfume of any flower.

It was the marvellous human distillation which is called great art. It was brilliant and it was fragrant at once and it was a human thing, a powerful and a delicate human thing, the dancing of

Pavlova

Pavlova. She used herself up completely in giving her dancing to the world. At the box-office men and women paid to buy a little of Pavlova's very soul, a real thing, irreplaceable when she had yielded it up to them. She died at last, because it was all yielded up, and for herself there was nothing left.

Let us consider for a moment one of the most extraordinary facts about her life — the amount of travelling she did. *Why* should Pavlova have gone all over the world, to all the small towns, provincial towns, "one-horse" towns? By all the rules, there was no need for her to have done it. She was a great star, internationally acclaimed. She could easily have limited her appearances to about forty performances a year — at a four-figure weekly salary.

How much *easier* it would have been for Pavlova, say, to have produced one new ballet each year for a fortnight's season only, in London, Paris, Berlin and New York. The annual "Pavlova" season would have been a social and theatrical event, eagerly looked forward to in the great capitals.

Or she might have made arrangements to appear in opera for stated short seasons, like a prima donna, and with all the réclame and salary she cared to ask for.

(168)

Thus she could have created an even greater prestige for herself than actually she enjoyed; and because she would have had time to make her own experiments in choreography, we might have had twenty great ballets like "Autumn Leaves" instead of only one composition of her own. She could have lived comfortably at Ivy House for most of the year and become a noted figure in London society. By making herself exclusive and putting on the airs of a theatrical *grande dame,* she could have earned even more kudos and money than she actually did.

Yet she went to Bundaberg and Kidderminster, Dayton (Ohio), Pforzheim, Llandudno, Sourabaya, Aberdeen, Costa Rico, Pernambuco, Shanklin (I. of W.), and Singapore.

She wanted the citizens of these towns and all the other fairly important but not metropolitan towns of the whole world to see her dance. She knew she had a marvellous gift. She wanted to show *everybody* in the world what a thing her dancing was. She did not want fame and she did not want money. She wanted to dance — and to dance for everybody in the world.

In dingy little theatres, with inadequate scenery

and hopeless orchestras playing out-of-date music, she danced on and on — this great world star — with her trivial and sentimental themes and their conventional music only too often the despair of anybody at all sophisticated: yet everywhere bringing a grandeur of emotion into the dingy theatres, to the dull provincial audiences; using trivial themes merely as a background for her own not-trivial work — transforming the sentiment of the themes into monumental tragedy, making prettiness into beauty, and interpreting mediocre music as though it were the harmony of the spheres and all the dancing universe lived in her blood.

Has there ever been another, can there ever be another such dancer?

CHAPTER VIII

A Chapter of Accidents

BEFORE describing Pavlova's repertoire of ballets and divertissements, I set down a few anecdotes describing what happened when things went wrong. Her career was singularly free from misadventure. Wherever she travelled, she seemed to miss earthquakes, cyclones, shipwrecks, revolutions, and other violent upheavals of man and nature. It was a belief seriously held by many members of her Company that Pavlova was under divine protection — or alternately, that she was in harmony with the forces of nature. Thus, it is a fact that she never had a rough Channel crossing, despite the most threatening of weather forecasts. Again, she often had very narrow escapes, as on the occasion in America when the train in which she was travelling passed over a bridge which collapsed *after* her carriage had crossed to the other side. All this may have been pure coincidence. We know that theatrical folk are superstitious. I merely state what the Company believed, and record the fact that if she was not divinely guided, then at any rate she was extraordinarily lucky.

She was in only two train accidents, to my knowledge. The first was in America, as mentioned above. The second was the railway accident in France, during which she caught the chill which led to her death. On this occasion, the express in which Pavlova was travelling crashed into a goods train and all the windows on one side were shattered. It was a corridor train and the glass was broken on the corridor side of the carriages, with the result that nobody was seriously injured. Pavlova was amused, after the excitement had died down slightly, to hear one of the members of her Company lamenting volubly in Russian that he would have to pay a fine because he had pulled the communication cord on hearing the crash. On dressing and emerging from his berth, he realized that a most serious accident had been very narrowly avoided. Whereupon he began to boast that it was surely his prompt action in pulling the cord which had brought the express to a standstill!

I do not remember any performance that had to

be cancelled through misadventure, or for any other reason, in all her strenuous career. Even on her deathbed, Anna Pavlova insisted that her Company should go on with the tour — which they did.

There was, however, one rather amusing occasion on which Pavlova walked off the stage and refused to continue with the performance. During her season in the Malay States the manager of one of the theatres had given permission to a photographer to go into the wings and take pictures of the dances. Now, Pavlova was particularly sensitive to the presence of outsiders or unauthorized strangers, and would never allow any one not connected with the performance to stand in the wings or even to be present at rehearsals. When she saw the intruder she at once walked off. The curtain came down and Madame would not resume until the photographer had left.

There was another occasion when the performance was interrupted, though it can scarcely be described as an accident. While we were in Glasgow, there was a choir of Cossacks in the town. The members came to our theatre in Russian costumes — impressively big men physically — brushed past the stage-doorkeeper and rushed on to the stage, actually while Pavlova was dancing a solo number. They surrounded her and presented her with flowers and tokens. The audience thought it was all part of the ballet. Pavlova was unnerved, as might have been expected by this unrehearsed occurrence. When she was dancing, she was in a kind of trance and it was nothing less than a severe nervous shock for her to be interrupted. She told me afterwards that what had horrified her most of all was, not so much the appearance of the Cossacks, as the fact that *they spoke to her*.

After so many years of work without words, the effect of people talking to her on the stage during a performance was to give her a severe shock.

In the category of mishaps, I must record something queer which happened the very last time that Pavlova danced in public — at Golders Green Hippodrome on the 13th day of December, 1930. I have previously mentioned that Pavlova never allowed anything but flowers to be handed up on to the stage at the end of the performance. On this occasion, the rule was broken. When she was taking her call with the whole Company, after the finale, a life-size statue of the Madonna with Child was incongruously carried on to the stage. I have

PAVLOVA IN PRIVATE LIFE

Pavlova

no idea from which of her admirers this unusual
tribute came; but it is a fact that the appearance
of the holy image on a stage surrounded by richly
costumed ballet girls was to some minds a breach of
taste. When the final curtain came down, Pavlova
remained looking at the statue for some minutes
with tears in her eyes, before turning to run wildly
to her dressing room. In the Company the incident
was regarded as a bad omen.

Pavlova herself regarded as a particularly bad
omen something that happened to her in Berlin
in 1913. She had, like a good pre-revolutionary
Russian, a superstitious awe of royalty, as such. After "Les Preludes" at the Kroll Opera House, she
was presented to the Kaiser and Kaiserin. The
Kaiserin extended her gloved hand to her. She
curtsied and kissed the white glove, leaving on it
a bright scarlet patch from her lip rouge. She was
terribly dismayed, more particularly when the
Kaiserin made a joke about "Blood" on her hands.
And when the War came, Pavlova could not be
convinced that the red stain of that evening was
anything other than an omen. This story has been
told about others, but it happened originally and
authentically to Pavlova.

(175)

Pavlova

About 1912, I was visiting Pavlova at Hampstead. We were chatting at the doorway and she had her left hand resting against the door jamb. A gust of wind blew the door shut. To my horror, I saw that three fingers of her hand were crushed. There was only a Russian maid in the house, who could understand very little English, but I managed to convey that hot water was urgently necessary. Pavlova was bearing the pain with fortitude. I had a fear that those wonderfully expressive fingers had been destroyed. I seized her arm and plunged her hand into the hot water. She screamed with fear of my rough-and-ready treatment rather than with the pain, though that must have been intense. The injury was so serious that for weeks she had to dance with one artificial finger attached to her hand, the damaged finger being doubled in against her palm.

An almost incredible instance of her courage in overcoming physical pain is the fact that on her last English tour (1930), Anna Pavlova actually suffered from an *injured kneecap!* Such a misfortune to a dancer can scarcely be imagined. The agony of an inflamed knee when balancing on the *point* and pirouetting as only Pavlova could pirou-

Pavlova

ette must have been almost beyond even her en-
durance. Yet she continued with her dancing. She
would not allow the tour to be cancelled.

Reality was to her essentially a matter of the
spirit. She applied this even to her pain. Deeply en-
grained in her fibres was the feeling that *she must
dance* — in any and every circumstance her con-
sciousness required this rhythmical bodily expression. The desire for this expression was so great
that body and spirit were one being and that being
could only live in the rapture of the dance.

There was once when Pavlova's limbs refused
to obey her spirit's compulsion to dance. It was at a
matinée and she was overworked and overworried.
Or perhaps merely she was suffering from that
form of emotional reaction which, particularly
among Russians, takes the form of an extreme melancholy. I began playing the "Gavotte Pavlova",
watching for her entrance. She did not appear. I
knew something was wrong and feared an accident. The piece was finished by the orchestra,
without any dance. I began it again. Then I got a
signal to stop and go on with the next divertissement, one in which Pavlova was not to take part.
I learned afterwards that she had remained in

her dressing room all through the "Gavotte", unable to collect herself for the dance, sobbing in a mood of dejection and apathy. Afterwards she asked me to come to her dressing room and she told me frankly that she was sorry for what had happened, but she could not explain what had come over her. "I was so miserable!" she said. That was all. She had recovered herself immediately after the "Gavotte", and in order to keep faith with the audience, she afterwards did an extra dance not announced in the programme.

On another occasion, she failed to make her entry for "The Swan." I played the piece right through, without Pavlova, and began it a second time. Halfway through, she entered and danced from that point to the end. The audience did not notice that anything was wrong. Actually Pavlova had danced in great pain. This was not a case of temperament. It was a nasty accident. Hurrying along from her dressing room, she had knocked herself against an iron girder behind the back cloth. The stage was not properly equipped with pilot lights. She had bruised her arm and her hip. When she had recovered from the first shock, she did not allow the mere pain to affect her dancing.

Pavlova

On one occasion in my early association with Anna Pavlova, before the War, on her second English tour, her partner Novikoff sprained his knee and could not dance. There was no substitute available and there was no time to rehearse with the orchestra any substitute divertissements for those in which Novikoff appeared. Pavlova decided to fill up the programme with several short dances solo, to the accompaniment of a piano in the wings. I played for her and Pavlova excelled herself in rising to the occasion. The audience, perhaps, realizing the circumstances, gave her a rapturous applause. She was so pleased and excited at having overcome the difficulties that she quite forgot everything. She dragged me, very much a blushing youth, out on the stage, threw her arms about my neck, and gleefully kissed me in front of the whole audience!

It was on the same tour, in Dublin, that part of the scenery collapsed and a "flat" fell from the wings on to Anna Pavlova. The audience gasped. Pavlova did not crawl from beneath the "flat." She emerged, still dancing with grace, as though nothing unrehearsed had happened. As she moved, she found means to improvise little gestures to pat her frock and her hair into position. In the dust still rising from the floor, she danced on and on, over the fallen piece of scenery, unconcerned. The Irish audience went wild with delight.

There was one occasion, in the years I have known her, that Anna Pavlova tripped and fell — through what, in a lesser dancer, would have been described bluntly as clumsiness! The stage was in semi-darkness and Pavlova stumbled and fell prostrate over one of the other dancers. But only the Company knew what had happened. She fell with such elegance that the audience had no idea that anything was amiss. As she fell, she said quietly in Russian to the others, "Keep still!" She rose effortlessly and the ballet went on. Always the ballet went on! That was Pavlova's religion, — that nothing can stop the dance.

At a theatre in Italy once the lights failed. The stage and the orchestra were in darkness, though the lights in the auditorium still threw a faint glimmer. I kept the orchestra playing from memory as well as they were able, and on the dim stage I could see the ballet moving with its usual precision. After a couple of minutes the lights came on again. The ballet was exactly in position to continue with the music, though it was a complicated *ensemble*.

I conclude this short chapter of accidents with a strange incident that occurred while we were in Spain. A fire broke out on the stage and the safety curtain came down with a rush. There was a moment of indecision and breathlessness in the auditorium. Then an imposing figure stood erect in the Royal Box. It was General Primo de Rivera, Dictator of Spain. In parade-ground tones he commanded the people to remain calm. They remained in their seats either through fear of the Dictator or from a desire to see more of Pavlova, I will not say which.

CHAPTER IX

Her Repertoire of Ballets

THE ballets which Pavlova selected for her performances were of the kind which, as she was enabled to judge from an ever-increasing experience, would most appeal to her audiences. It must be remembered that Pavlova was not an experimentalist in the same sense as Serge Diaghiliev, seeking new developments in the art of the ballet itself. She was a missionary of the art of ballet dancing. Her performances were not confined to centres of culture — London, Paris, Berlin, New York. She went into the outposts of civilization, not as a *reformist* of the art of ballet, but as an *exponent* of the art of ballet. When Pavlova went to small provincial towns, or to Australia, or to the agricultural areas of the United States, she would quite likely have failed completely with, for example, a ballet *à la* Diaghiliev to the music of Stravinsky. Pavlova's repertoires were selected to please a world public and not the hypercritical sophisticated public of the metropolitan centres. Even in London the Diaghiliev public and the Pavlova public were entirely different. The Diaghiliev audiences were more "intellectual" and the Pavlova audiences more "sentimental", if this distinction is valid.

It was because, in many places where Pavlova danced, such a thing as ballet had never been seen before, that she had actually to be careful not to become the victim of the laughter of Philistines. Undoubtedly she would have liked to have made Metropolitan experiments, but her experiences even in Europe were not so encouraging. By the time the War came, and the beginning of the "modern" movement in art, Pavlova was already established as a favourite in classical rôles. I remember her disappointment when, in Berlin in 1912, she produced on original lines "The Three Palms" to the music of Spendiarov with many new or mildly revolutionary departures from her established methods. Although her own dancing was superlatively lauded, the ballet itself failed to evoke either from critics or the public the enthusiasm which she had hoped. It was the same with her ballet "Adjanta Frescoes", in which she went to the ancient Hindu mythology for her inspiration in gestures and abstract forms, quite in advance of post-War art vogues. The public thought of her as the Swan, or as the Fairy Doll, or as the classical sylph dancing to Chopin's music. Even Novikoff's fine ballet, "Russian Folk Lore", to Tscherepnine's music, did not succeed as it deserved and as she hoped it would.

Gradually Pavlova came to realize that the public was right and that modernism in art did not suit her. Therefore she remained, all through the upheavals of æsthetic coteries, a classical "back number." Through all the periods of syncopation and steam-engines in music, she continued to dance Strauss waltzes and Chopin mazurkas. Curiously enough, she was vindicated just before her death by the return to popularity of the old rhythms in the latest ballroom dancing and the virtual collapse of jazz, even in cabarets.

Critics who, five years ago, could have spoken superciliously of Pavlova as a "back number" might be themselves considered out of date if they gave expression to the same æsthetic dogmatism in the year 1931. It is now becoming fashionable to

PAVLOVA WITH LAURENT NOVIKOFF IN ONE OF HER LAST
APPEARANCES AT THE MANHATTAN OPERA HOUSE

be pre-War in taste. To all intents and purposes, Pavlova was never anything else throughout the whole of her career.

I once heard her say to a critic, "Are you for me or for Diaghiliev?" The critic, with a wit uncommon in his profession, answered at once, "Both, Madame." At which reply, Pavlova was not displeased. She knew there was no essential antagonism between her type of ballet and that produced by Diaghiliev, and that it was only a carping criticism which tried to praise or disparage one in contrast with the other. The reason that Pavlova originally left Diaghiliev was that she was too great an individualist to be used merely for the expression of other people's ideas. Had she remained with Diaghiliev she would have become famous, none the less, but it was not the ambition for fame which caused her to take her own line. She felt that she had reached that point in her career when she had to make her own gesture to the world, no matter what the difficulties. She knew that by the power of her own art she could enthrall audiences, even without a brilliant supporting Company, without gorgeous and new *décor* (such as those used by Diaghiliev in the "Firebird"). Her confidence was justified because although Pavlova's Company included only one star of the first magnitude — herself — and although her stage settings for the most part were not daringly "modern" in design, yet she never achieved anything less than the greatest success possible in the theatre.

I have said that she was a missionary, spreading the very idea of ballet in remote parts of the earth. Naturally, the themes which she chose were those which would have the widest popular or sentimental appeal. She knew perfectly well what she was doing. It would have been absurd to say that she was *pandering* to popular taste, because, in fact, she was *educating* the popular taste wherever she went, both musically and æsthetically, by her practical demonstration that the ballet is an art form of unlimited potentialities.

She did not religiously follow the exact scheme of the older ballets, and very often a ballet danced by Pavlova under the name of one of the classical favourites, such as "La Fille Mal Gardée", "The "Fairy Doll", or "Don Quixote", and even "Giselle", had been very considerably altered to suit her purposes or her caprice. Given the choreography of a traditional ballet, she could not rest

(186)

until she had introduced variations and generally new music by another composer, making a choreographic and musical patchwork which charmed audiences, but could not fail to annoy those who realized what she had done. All things considered, however, I am inclined to think that she improved every ballet she revised. It was merely irritating musically to have sudden transitions from the music of Glazounow to that of Drigo in such a ballet as "Amarilla."

I was never quite able to decide how much of the responsibility for these alterations was Pavlova's and how much was due to her choreographers. When a ballet was specially arranged for Pavlova by Fokine or Clustine or Chiriaieff or Pianowski or Novikoff, they naturally wanted to display her to the best advantage. But after they had done their work, Pavlova would never let well alone, and would make further alterations and adaptations until the ballet suited her.

It is in this sense that she was artistically creative. The ballets danced by Pavlova were distinctively hers, her creation, despite the traditional title and settings. In giving below a brief description of some of the ballets in her repertoire, I should like

to draw attention more particularly to her versatility. In the preparation of each of these dance-
dramas, there was a tremendous amount of de-
tailed work, forethought, and knowledge involved, besides merely interpretative ability. The
manœuvres of a regiment of Guards trooping the
colours are simple, in comparison with the manœuvres of the *corps-de-ballet*.

I shall describe briefly about twenty of her
characteristic ballets. In each of them she had several solo dances and variations to remember, besides her movement in the ensembles. Her repertoire of dances was undoubtedly more extensive
than that of any dancer who has ever lived. Taglione had nothing like the versatility of Pavlova.
She had one rôle — the classical danseuse —
whereas Pavlova had everything from that to
Mexican, Hindu, Egyptian, fantastic, comic,
tragic, sentimental and realistic parts to dance.
Her repertoire covered all periods of history and
costume and mannerism.

I set down a brief description of some of her
ballets, hoping to illustrate this point in particular:
that although she was a classical danseuse in the
strictest sense of the term, yet her versatility was

such that it could fairly be claimed that she broadened and deepened the classical idea itself.

La Fille Mal Gardée

MUSIC: Hertel, with two variations by Delibes.
CHOREOGRAPHY: Petipa.

This is one of the classic Russian ballets, originally danced by Pavlova in two acts, but later adapted as a complete ballet in one act. The music and the dancing provided her with an opportunity to display coquettish and gay miming. As Lisa, the mischievous daughter of the tyrant mother who kept her under lock and key in order to arrange a marriage of convenience, Pavlova gave a character portrayal full of vivacity. There were moments of delicious light comedy, as when Lisa tantalises and teases the stupid son of a wealthy neighbour to whom she is plighted unwillingly. There were moments of tender sentiment and romance, as when Lisa and her true love, Colin, dance the "Pas de Ruban", in which a long ribbon winds the sweethearts symbolically together. The happy ending comes when the tyrant mother herself inadvertently locks Lisa and Colin together in a

(189)

hayloft, so compromising the "badly guarded daughter", on the very day arranged for her marriage of convenience. The stupid rival of Colin vanishes heavenwards, borne up by his own open umbrella during a storm — a moment of broad comedy which invariably delighted audiences.

Musically, it was the addition of the two variations by Delibes, a Pizzicato and an Adagio (the latter a charming viola solo) which redeemed the ballet. For the rest, only Pavlova's effervescent personality could have overcome the poverty of ideas in the music.

The Fairy Doll

MUSIC: Bayer, with variations by other composers.
CHOREOGRAPHY: Clustine.

This ballet was always a favourite with the public. It is essentially a pretty theme, based on sheer fantasy. Anna Pavlova danced as the fairy doll, the pride of the toymaker, who could not be induced to part with her until eventually he is persuaded by the offer of a large sum of money from a wealthy Englishman — who, by the way, was always dressed as a Scotchman! — and arranges to deliver her next day. That evening the fairy doll dances her farewell to the other dolls in the shop, who come stiffly to life to say farewell to her in their turn.

The *motif* of this ballet was a Fairy Doll Waltz. No one who has seen this ballet could ever forget the picture of Anna Pavlova when she came down from her cardboard box, three steps, to begin shyly dancing, in a dainty rhythm, her fairy doll waltz to music so quietly played that it could scarcely be heard. As she was revealed from behind her curtain, a gasp of amazement would be heard from the auditorium. There was also a variation to a xylophone solo, very lively, expressing the precise and neat beauty of the doll; and there was an Adagio of tender farewell to Drigo's music — in which she astounded audiences by her balancing on the *point, en arabesque*.

The xylophone solo presented difficulties, as in some places visited the only instrument available was not in the correct pitch. Consequently I would have to do without a xylophone and play an orchestral version of the variation.

Anna Pavlova was always disappointed when this contingency arose, as the clear hard tones of the xylophone expressed the precision and filigree work of her dance.

Amarilla

MUSIC: Glazounow and Drigo.
CHOREOGRAPHY: Clustine.

In this ballet Pavlova revealed her superb histrionic abilities, in the tragic rôle of the gypsy girl asked to dance at a festival in honour of a count who had formerly been her lover, on the occasion of his betrothal to a lady of rank and title. She dances with abandon, hoping to win him back; but her only reward is a purse of gold. She falls senseless to the ground, in bafflement and despair.

I have referred elsewhere to Anna Pavlova's histrionic powers, and no one who has seen "Amarilla" will dispute that she was one of the world's greatest actresses, quite apart from her genius as a dancer. Her acting was not a matter of mime and stereotyped movement. It was inspired and alive with passionate fervour. With every gesture she won pity for the drab gypsy, dancing with a heart breaking before the slightly tolerant assembly of aristocrats. As the little, crushed figure fell sobbing to the floor, one felt that all the hopeless love in the world had found its expression at that moment. The ballet showed, too, how little of Pavlova's artistic effects were achieved by the aid of costume. The drab gypsy girl was outshone in every way by the brilliant company; but inside those drab clothes was a personality who electrified all beholders with her dynamic power of emotional expression. Her three solo dances in this ballet were an Adagio (*pas de deux*), a Valse, and a Galop (all by Drigo). Especially electrifying was her *pas de bourré,* while moving backwards, with loosely hanging hands and arms and backward bent head and body, expressing at once deep emotion and lost hope of love.

The first part of the ballet was by Glazounow. One could easily tell the point where his music stopped and that of Drigo began.

Autumn Leaves

Music: Chopin.
Choreography: Anna Pavlova.

This is the only complete ballet designed and arranged by Pavlova herself. For poetry of line it

Pavlova

was unexcelled by any other in her repertoire. It is the answer to those who say that Anna Pavlova was not an inventive genius. Considering its success, one can only be amazed that she never turned her attention more to the choreographic aspect of her work.

"Autumn Leaves" is a choreographic poem describing the passing of the seasons, and the decline and death of nature in the year's cycle. The scene is a wood lit by the weak rays of an autumn sun and swept by the North Wind, which scatters the falling leaves, lifting them from the ground and sending them dancing and swirling through the air. The Chrysanthemum flower (Pavlova), the last bloom of the season, falls to the ground as a poet, book in hand, comes strolling through the wood. He picks up the flower, smooths its petals, and seeks to revive it. But the North Wind snatches the flower from his hand. Children come to play in the wood. The Chrysanthemum is slowly buried and forgotten beneath the whirling leaves.

One notices immediately the tenderness of this conception, and how it is suited for the finest choreographic effects. The groupings and ensembles as designed by Pavlova were expressive of the theme in terms of the highest possible achievement of the art of the ballet.

She showed, too, considerable discernment in selecting the music of Chopin, the Nocturnes with their sad pleading appeal aptly expressing the spirit of autumn. Pavlova herself danced solos to the "D Flat Major Nocturne" and the middle part of the "Fantaisie Impromptu." She was fond of Chopin's music, which was used in another ballet ("Chopiniana") to be described later.

Before the curtain went up for the performance of "Autumn Leaves", Pavlova never failed to rehearse the ballet, no matter how well it had been rehearsed that morning. These last-minute rehearsals continued until only a few minutes before the performance proper began.

Snowflakes

MUSIC: Tschaikowski.
CHOREOGRAPHY: Clustine.

Musically, this was one of Pavlova's best ballets. Tschaikowski's music, including parts of the "Casse Noisette" suite, was so melodic and colourful, and the numbers so well linked together, that the music went from strength to strength. Appreciation of the dance does not demand any story-reference, as the ballet was a theme rather than an episode, with a musical rather than a dramatic climax. After an overture, the curtain goes up to reveal a wintry scene with a purple glow in the background and a misty glacier-green light. The Ballet, dressed to symbolise snowflakes, gambol and whirl to a valse. The Queen of the Snowflakes (Pavlova) enters and dances an Adagio (with partner). There follows a *pas de trois,* a *pas de quatre* (men), a *pas de cinq,* and two variations, one danced by Pavlova, and the coda danced by Pavlova and her partner with an ensemble in which the Queen of the Snowstorm is held aloft in air, while the drifts whirl around her. The whole was a pure interpretation of music in the dance.

Don Quixote

Music: Minkus.

Choreography: Novikoff (after the Classical Ballet).

An opportunity was lost here of producing a really historic work. The theme, the stage settings, the dancing, were all adapted for a ballet

PAVLOVA IN "SNOWFLAKES"

par excellence, but when I say that the music was
utterly undistinguished, I flatter it. The dull, stupid
tunes of Minkus, who was nothing more than a
"hack" composer, completely ruined Novikoff's
choreography and even Pavlova's Spanish dancing. Music could scarcely be more sickly and maud-
lin than the stuff used in this ballet to suggest a
love episode. It is to be regretted that so much time,
money, and thought should have been wasted by
the revival of a ballet with music which could not
have been worse for the purpose. Novikoff was
driven almost to distraction by its banality.

Despite this drawback, the ballet was fairly well
received, even in the Latin-American countries and
in Spain. This was because of the interest and hu-
mour of the theme. The ballet is in two acts. In
the first, Pavlova danced the part of Kitry, an inn-
keeper's daughter at Barcelona. Don Quixote, rid-
ing on a scraggy nag and accompanied by Sancho
Panza on a donkey, come into the market place
where there is a gay festival. Sancho Panza is tossed
in a blanket by the revellers, and there is a fight
between Don Quixote and Kitry's lover, Basilio.
Basilio feigns to be stabbed, and Kitry expresses
her anguish. In Act II, Don Quixote and Sancho,

on their journey through the forest, wearily fall asleep. The Don dreams that he fights with a knight in armour, but is defeated; and as a compensation Dulcinea (Pavlova) invests him with a resplendent Order of Chivalry.

It will be realized from this description what an opportunity for miming and dancing such a theme gives. Alas that the opportunity was spoiled by the use of such trivial music! Tscherepnine rescored "Don Quixote", and what Tscherepnine does not know about orchestration is not worth knowing. All that was possible to do, he did, but a bad tune remains a bad tune, notwithstanding the finest orchestration.

Dionysius

MUSIC: Tscherepnine.
CHOREOGRAPHY: Clustine.

The music of this ballet was written specially for Pavlova. There was only one line of thought in the score, and consequently a satisfactory feeling of cohesion.

The stage setting is an ancient Greek Temple of Dionysius. The High Priestess (Pavlova) in a trance invokes the god, and his statue comes to life and dances with her. A wild bacchanalian orgy follows, increasing in intensity and frenzy. The god returns to his pedestal, and the High Priestess, disconsolate, supplicates him to return to life, but in vain. It will be noted that the theme is phallic and orgiastic, in the sense of the Eleusinian mysteries of the Greeks, related to the origins and worship of life itself. How utterly different to the "pretty-pretty" themes of such ballets as "The Fairy Doll", which the public loved! Here we saw Pavlova in a frenzy of abandon, nothing cold or precise, but frankly expressing sex in art, though without any grotesqueness or degradations of the conception of orgy. In this Pavlova showed the contrast between her own art, and that of Isadora Duncan. The latter was devoted to Dionysius as a cult. Pavlova included the god in her repertoire.

Invitation to the Valse

MUSIC: Weber.
CHOREOGRAPHY: Zaylich.

The setting is a ballroom of the early Victorian period with the women in crinolines. Pavlova takes the rôle of a debutante, appropriately coy. Before her entry, the Company dances in the manner of the period. She enters shyly and does a variation to a movement from one of Weber's early sonatas. The two gallants contend for her hand. She coquettes with them both, without showing preference for either — a subtle piece of miming. At last she is whirled away to the seductive music of the well-known "Invitation to the Valse." The atmosphere of the ballet is dignified and restrained until the music of the valse proper, which for the debutante becomes a crescendo of thrills, as she abandons herself to the music. The ballet is conceived in a conventional style. It was interesting for Pavlova's psychological study of the blushing young girl "coming out." The orchestration of "The Invitation to the Valse" was by Berlioz.

Walpurgis Night

MUSIC: Gounod.
CHOREOGRAPHY: Clustine.

This is a ballet from "Faust", not generally danced in the operatic performances. The title "Walpurgis Night" is somewhat of a misnomer, as the scene is Greek, with Pavlova as Helen of Troy; and not the conventional Witches' Sabbath. The theme is based on the interlude in which Mephistopheles takes Faust, in order to distract his thoughts from Marguerite, to a phantom world of ancient Greece, and a meeting with Helen of Troy.

In costuming and choreography, the ballet is a blend of the Hellenic and the Egyptian. Rising on a darkened stage, the curtain revealed a brief outline glimpse, in silhouette, of a wild craggy region. Then, with the raising of an intervening gauze curtain, the scene changes to a Greek temple with slaves in attendance upon Helen of Troy. There were two solos danced by Pavlova, the more brilliant being that in which Faust gives her a casket of jewels. The music of Gounod is well enough known not to require any further comment here.

Chopiniana

A SUITE OF DANCES TO THE MUSIC OF CHOPIN:

1. Polonaise in A major.
2. Prelude in A flat.
3. Valse in C sharp minor (arranged by Fokine).

4. Valse in A minor.
5. Prelude in A major.
6. Mazurka in C major.
7. Valse in A flat major.
8. Valse in F major.
CHOREOGRAPHY: Clustine.

Although this ballet was one of those without a "story" appeal, being merely a suite of dances in the classical method with dancers in three-quarter length ballet skirts and the men in white tights and small black velvet jackets, it was a favourite everywhere we went. The music had been well selected for dancing, and although each number was complete in itself, an impression was achieved, so well were the numbers linked together, of a continuous performance — more so, perhaps, than in any ballet she did.

Anna Pavlova's dances were a *pas de deux* (Number 3), a solo (Number 5), and a variation in the ensemble (Number 8). This was one of the few ballets that could be done without scenery, and was equally effective against a background of plain dark curtains as with the moonlit scene, or the Versailles garden, which were sometimes used.

PAVLOVA IN "CHOPINIANA"

Pavlova
The Three Palms

Music: Spendiarov.
Choreography: Fokine.

This ballet was also known by another name — "The Seven Daughters." The story describes the visit of an Oriental Prince, with his entourage, to the Court of another Potentate, who has seven daughters. Despite their father's commands, six of the daughters engage in revelry with the visitors, and as a punishment are put to death by fire. The seventh daughter (Pavlova) is enamoured of the visiting Prince, but her father will not give his consent to a marriage. After the Prince and his retinue have gone away, the seventh daughter comes to a fountain in the garden on a moonlight night. She leans against the fountain, and as the jet of water gradually subsides, we see her dying of a broken heart.

As a ballet, "The Three Palms" was distinctive — too much so. Choreography and music were like a piece of mosaic, so inseparable was one from the other. The stage setting, the dress, and the colour, gave an effect of "The Arabian Nights."

Pavlova's Oriental dancing calls for a special

(203)

comment. Either because she was a Russian, or merely because she was a very great artist, she was able to represent the spirit of the West and the spirit of the East with equal profundity of insight. Nothing could be more European than her ballroom dancing in such ballets as "Invitation to the Waltz", and in divertissements such as "The Gavotte Pavlova." Yet in her Oriental ballets and in "The Syrian Dance", she became completely transformed and one had an irresistibly Oriental effect. Her spiral movements, her voluptuous poses and undulations, and the sensuous Eastern expression of her face were as un-European as could be. At such times one felt that she was in her person the Russian enigma — an expression in art of that strange balance which Russians hold between the European and the Asiatic mind. Anna Pavlova had perhaps some Tartar blood in her, as many Russians have, and it may have been this which gave her such an instinctively strong feeling of genuineness as she danced her Eastern numbers.

At the time of the production of "The Three Palms", at the Kroll Opera House in Berlin, I saw Spendiarov frequently. He told me that when he wrote the music, he worked with a turban on his head in order to feel the atmosphere of the East!

Visions

Music: Tschaikowski.
Choreography: Clustine.

Based on Perrault's fable, this ballet was originally to music by Tschaikowski under the title of "The Sleeping Beauty" — a big ballet in four acts. Pavlova used one act, the episode where the fairy appears to the prince lost in the wood while out hunting, and shows him a vision of the Sleeping Beauty (Pavlova) with whom he at once falls in love.

This is the first ballet which Anna Pavlova saw when, as a child, her mother took her to the Mariansky Theatre.

The Magic Flute

Music: Drigo.
Choreography: Petipa.

Whoever hears the playing of the Magic Flute must dance! Luc, a young countryman, who finds a decrepit fop of a marquis likely to carry off the pretty Lise (Pavlova), owing to the greed of Lise's mother, befriends an old hermit, who is really Oberon, and receives from him the magic instrument. He plays it to Lise and she is compelled to dance until she drops in exhaustion. It is next tried on the interfering mother, on the decrepit marquis, on the gendarmes who come to arrest Luc; and finally the judge and the whole court of law are set skipping with various degrees of nimbleness. Luc is condemned to death for sorcery, but Oberon discloses his identity and everything is set right.

This is one of the ballets in which the audience could be assured of a hearty laugh, as it is full of the spirit of fun and pranks all through. The music is light ballet music at its best. One does not tire of "The Magic Flute", as the action on the stage never flags from beginning to end.

The Egyptian Mummy

MUSIC: Tscherepnine.
CHOREOGRAPHY: Clustine.

A traveller goes to Egypt and sees the mummy of a former Queen in one of the tombs. He asks the guide if he may stay there one night, but the guide warns him that it is dangerous to do so. He comes back, however, and is overcome with sleep. He dreams that the sarcophagus opens, and the Queen dressed in white comes out to him. She gives signs that she knows him, that they met in a former incarnation.

The scene changes in the dream to thousands of years ago. She was one of the Pharaoh's daughters and he was a High Priest. A big festival is being celebrated, during which she manages to drop a lotus in front of the High Priest, who picks it up reverently and returns it to her. She reveals that she loves him. One of the other priests has seen them together, and reports this to the Pharaoh, who orders their separation and their death. She begs for mercy for the Priest; this is granted him, but she must die. Pharaoh orders the poison, which both take and die.

Change of scene again to the sarcophagus. The traveller awakes and rushes to the tomb and finds it closed. As he stands there distracted, he sees the sarcophagus open and the Queen lying in the mummy case. He kisses her. When the guide comes later, he finds the traveller's dead body.

I have stated this theme rather extensively to show the subtleties of mime necessary in conveying such a story to an audience in dumb show. Pavlova's dance as Pharaoh's daughter was made with conventionalized Egyptian gestures, but in a peculiarly intense manner, which had the effect of bringing ancient mysteries into life again. For many of her gestures in this ballet, she copied exactly the attitudes which she learned after a close study of original Egyptian papyri and stélés.

Adjanta Frescoes

MUSIC: Tscherepnine *fils*.
CHOREOGRAPHY: Clustine.

From the point of view of scholarship and original research, this is one of the most interesting of her ballets. While she was in India she visited the temple at Adjanta and made careful notes, drawings and photographs of the frescoes there. She then worked out with Clustine a suite of dances, making use of the authentic attitudes of the frescoes. Tscherepnine's music was an attempt to convey Hindu mysticism. Because her public could not understand the intention of the piece, Pavlova reluctantly abandoned it. There was too much abstract dancing to please an audience and not enough drama.

Oriental Impressions

MUSIC: Uday-Shankar.

CHOREOGRAPHY: Comolsta Banerjü.

On her first tour to India and the Far East, Pavlova conceived the idea of an Oriental ballet. The result was this — a composite Oriental effect, beginning with a Japanese dance with geisha girls and a comic interlude by male dancers. The second scene opens with a Hindu wedding, including a dance by eight nautch girls. The ballet ended with a little devotional piece, "Krishna and Rada", in which Pavlova worships Shri Krishna, bringing flowers and gifts to him as he plays his flute; after which they dance together. It is not a little remarkable that Pavlova should have danced this ballet in India before an audience consisting of Hindus appreciative of the subtler points of technique and interpretation. It says much for her technical powers and her capacity to study detail minutely that invariably the Hindu critics were delighted with her performance.

Pavlova
Les Préludes

Music: Liszt.

Choreography: Fokine.

The theme is taken from Lamartine's "Poetic Meditations" with more particular reference to the passage which may be freely translated as follows:

"What is our life but a series of Preludes to that unknown hymn of which death strikes the first solemn note? Love is at the enchanted dawn of our lives; but in every one's destiny the first thrills of happiness are interrupted sooner or later by the breath of a storm which scatters lovely illusions, which destroys the altar with a fatal thunderbolt. There is no soul, be it ever so cruelly battered, which after one of these tempests cannot seek to find solace in the gentle peace of life in the countryside. Yet man cannot properly resign himself for any length of time to the enjoyment of the benevolent lassitude which charms him at first in the bosom of nature. When the trumpets sound the call to battle, he hastens to a dangerous outpost in whatever War may happen to summon him to its trenches, in order that he may find in struggle a fuller knowledge of himself and the entire enjoyment of his power."

It was to this theme that Liszt wrote his "Symphonic Poem Number 3," which music was used by Fokine for what might be termed a philosophical ballet, especially arranged for the most poetical of all dancers — Anna Pavlova.

Pavlova was entranced with the theme. It has often been remarked that the peculiar quality of her dancing is poetic frailty as opposed to mere muscular virtuosity. Here she had an opportunity (which was only bettered in one other of her ballets, "Autumn Leaves") to give an expression to the nature-mysticism which formed such a pronounced element in her. The poetical philosophy of Lamartine expresses more nearly than anything else in literature precisely what was distinctive in the dancing of Anna Pavlova. The dreamy, poetically mournful, fatalistic view of life was naturally hers. It will be remarked how many of her dances gave expression to this pathetic fatalism. Apart from the stories of frustrated love in "Giselle", "Amarilla", "The Egyptian Mummy", and "The Three Palms", there is the same note of sadness in the scattering of the petals of the last

chrysanthemum in "Autumn Leaves" — a homage
to inexorable death, which can, nevertheless, be
death beautiful. "Chopiniana", that dance of
ethereal sylphs, also gives the onlooker a feeling
of experiencing a beautiful but spectral vision. One
knew that, at the first light of dawn, those dreamy,
graceful figures would fade and disappear.

In "The Swan", her homage to Death is shown
at its most lucid moment in all her dancing. What
moved audiences more than any other element in
this dance was the sadness of her shining eyes as the
white bird died — a sadness which made the Swan
a symbol of all mortality.

So, in "Les Préludes", one had immediately a
plastic expression of what Lamartine meant by the
inexorable call of destiny — the weary spirit of
life, battered by storms, soothing itself with the
balm of Nature; then eager again for the struggle
and dashing into the centre of strife in order to
realize its powers of action.

The poetical mysticism which made Pavlova
unique among dancers found in "Les Préludes"
its most sustained expression; but it was too abstract, too mournful for the happy-go-lucky pre-
War audiences. I have often thought it is a pity

this ballet was not revived after the War, when it would have been in the strongest possible contrast with such deliberately pessimistic works as Stravinsky's "Les Noces." Pavlova's mournfulness, because it was a poetic mournfulness, was a truer artistic expression of æsthetic pessimism than the more obvious attempts at realism of so many movements in modern art.

Paquita

MUSIC: Delverez.

This was a suite of classical Spanish dances included in the repertoire of the Mariansky Theatre. When we were in South America, Madame Smirnova, who had been a ballerina in Russia, reconstructed the movements from memory, as some of the citizens of Buenos Aires had expressed the desire to see a revival of the grand manner in Spanish dancing as opposed to the popular styles with their inordinate use of heel-stamping and castanets. This ballet is, therefore, of interest purely as a grand *pas classique*. Although the atmosphere was Spanish, and the dancing Spanish, the costumes were the classical ballet skirts. The chief movements in the suite were an *entrée,* a big *adagio,* variations in the ensemble for Pavlova, and the *coda.* Here again, as in the "Adjanta Frescoes", Pavlova showed her audacity, in dancing, before critical audiences, something which although typical did not conform to type. All Spaniards love dancing, and the usual Spanish dancing, with its continual stamping and snapping of castanets, is in very great contrast with the airiness and daintiness of the classical court ballet. Yet in Buenos Aires and also in Spain, where she danced "Paquita", her reception was uproariously enthusiastic.

Russian Folk Lore

MUSIC: Tscherepnine.
CHOREOGRAPHY: Novikoff

As a typical and genuinely Russian number based on a traditional Russian tale, it might have been expected that audiences everywhere would have been keenly interested in this unusual ballet.

The action takes place in the Czar's palace, with the Czar in a mood of melancholy. Dancing girls endeavor to arouse him, but without effect. Court jesters do their capers, without avail. Three girls are brought in for the Czar to choose a lady love. They dance alluringly before him — and he falls asleep, bored. A dancing bear is brought to the palace and the Czar snores more loudly — until, at length, he awakens, and begins smashing the furniture! A magician enters, bringing Negro dancers and servants, with a magic book. The magician casts spells which cause the Negroes to dance with the bear. Then to the amazement of everybody, a voice is heard singing — a most beautiful voice, very high and clear. A magic bird (Pavlova) enters and begins flying hither and thither — piteously, because she is bound in chains. The Czar dashes forward and releases her from her bonds, whereupon, to his consternation, she flies away! Happily, he finds one of her feathers on the floor, The magician tells him to break it. This action breaks the spell and the magic bird returns in the guise of a beautiful princess who had been bewitched. The Czar marries the Princess and everybody lives happily ever afterwards.

"Russian Folk Lore" was richly conceived. The use of a singer (off stage) was unusual in a Pavlova ballet. One can only abuse the stupidity of audiences who could not realize that here was something outstanding — brilliantly so. Audiences who preferred hackneyed and trivial stuff like "The Fairy Doll" were lucky that Anna Pavlova ever gave them anything original at all!

A Polish Wedding

MUSIC: Krupinski.
CHOREOGRAPHY: Pianowski.

Pavlova never stopped adding to her repertoire. After the Declaration of Polish Independence, which was the outcome of the Great War, there was a convention at Warsaw of people from all the districts of Poland attired in the costumes, traditional and historical, of the countryside. This event gave Pianowski (himself a Pole) the inspiration for a brilliant little ballet representing a wedding festival in one of the remote villages of Poland. The music is entirely based upon the lively Polish folk melodies, and includes a brilliant *pas de trois,* a Polish mazurka, besides other folk dances.

Ethnologically, this little ballet is of the greatest interest and the whole conception and execution of it was pleasing.

Giselle

MUSIC: Adam.
CHOREOGRAPHY: Petipa.

The story of this great classical ballet is that of a girl driven by frustrated love to madness and death — an Ophelia of the dance — who later rises by magic from the grave to dance as a wraith before her remorseful lover.

A young village girl is in love with a Prince, who, in disguise, has courted her. Owing to a dramatic and unexpected visit to the village of the Princess who was affianced to Giselle's lover, Giselle discovers at the same time his identity and the fact that she must lose him forever. She cannot believe it. The proof is when a young boy from the village brings the sword and mantle of the Prince, which he had discarded before assuming his disguise to court her. Under the emotional strain she loses her reason. She takes the sword and looks at it with fascination. Then begins her mad dance, quietly at first, increasing in intensity of hysteria.

(217)

There is a pause, as though she had momentarily regained her reason. At this moment she appears to be communing with herself, as she realises her secret dreams. She dances vacantly a few steps which she had so recently danced with her lover. For a brief period she regains her reason. But this moment of sanity only warps her reason the more, and when she suddenly finds herself with a sword in her hand she decides to kill herself but is prevented by those around her. The cup of emotion is overfull. She dies of heartbreak.

In the second act we see her grave. The Prince strews flowers on it, kneels and prays that she should come back to him. The Queen of the Fairies with her attendant sprites listens to his prayer and makes the spirit of Giselle to rise from the grave. He dances with her spirit. The Fairy Queen orders her sprites to surround him and separate him from Giselle. As the light of dawn comes into the forest, the fairies disappear. Giselle remains, but she, too, gradually fades and sinks back into her grave, leaving the Prince alone. So great is his sorrow that he too dies.

Thus simply outlined, the story of "Giselle" may seem simple enough, but as Pavlova danced it,

Pavlova

it was not simple. When this ballet was announced
in the programme, every member of the Company wished it were not so. Anna Pavlova herself
was utterly exhausted, both mentally and physically, after each performance of "Giselle." Even
the most hardened playgoer was brought to tears
by the pathos of the scene where she lost her
reason and then took the sword, wonderingly and
caressingly, and danced with it. In the second act
her awakening from the enclosing grave was ter-
rifying, a moment of eerie suspense in a scene, dim
and mystic, which made one tremble with a fear
of the unknowable secrets of immortality. When
gradually she shook the chill of death from her
limbs and began her dance as a disembodied spirit,
so great was Pavlova's art that she seemed to —
and perhaps she did — leave the stage and float in
air. It was more than dancing, more than miming
or acting. It was a transfiguration.

With "Giselle", we may close this brief survey
of her repertoire of ballets. I do not say that "Giselle" was the greatest of her ballets, though it was
probably the one she liked best. My own preference
was for those which were musically consistent, such

as "Snowflakes" and "Dionysius", "Autumn
Leaves" and "Chopiniana." If music is to be allied to the graceful gestures and movements of
dancers, then the music itself should at least be
homogeneous in any one ballet. Pavlova never
subordinated herself to the music. She never regarded herself merely as an executant.

The music which she used to accompany her
dancing was good, if one considers it from a popular level, but it might have been ever so much better. She never danced to the music of Beethoven
and Wagner, Mozart, Glück or Bach — though
in fairness it should be recorded that she would
listen to me playing over the three last-named composers by the hour, wistfully saying that she wished
she could dance to them all. Why she did not
dance Beethoven (except for the Kreisler "Rondino") or Wagner, I cannot attempt to explain.
Those who know music will understand. In her
selection of music she had to bear in mind its
suitability for dancing, rather than its musical
quality as such. The simple rhythms and the
marked melodies suited her best. A glance at the
selections used in "Chopiniana" makes this point
clear.

Pavlova

I come back to the point stated in the beginning of this chapter, — that her selection of a repertoire of ballets was determined by her understanding of what the public could appreciate — a world public — and we can but marvel at the balance she was able to maintain between concessions to public taste and standards of musical excellence.

Her preference was for Romantic music, because the poetical side of her nature required romance. She was not an artistic revolutionary. If I played ultra-modern works to her, she would merely say "Why do composers want to say *ugly* things in their music? Music should express the beautiful things in life. That is why we have music."

A fine melody appealed to her more than the most exciting of rhythms. When the two were combined, as in Glazounow's "Bacchanale", Pavlova was impelled irresistibly to dance at her very best.

Though not a revolutionary, she was in her way an experimentalist. It was the public demand which made her keep on presenting old ballets such as "La Fille Mal Gardée" and "The Fairy Doll." She tried to redeem the musical poverty of these works by adding musical numbers by such composers as Glazounow, and Delibes, but this merely made more obvious the poverty of ideas in the original work. She proved herself an experimentalist, too, by producing ballets to the music of Chopin, Liszt, Glazounow, Tschaikowski, Spendiarov, and Tscherepnine; but of these only the Chopin ballets ("Chopiniana" and "Autumn Leaves") could really be described as having appealed to the public — as ballets, that is, apart from Pavlova's personal work, which never failed to please, no matter what she danced, whether to good or bad music. The public did not pay to see a new ballet, brilliantly conceived. The Pavlova public wanted to see Pavlova.

Far from being stereotyped in her work, she never ceased to search for something that would be new, without being, as she phrased it, "ugly." She was always extending her repertoire. Her productions of "Les Préludes", "The Three Palms", "Dionysius", "The Egyptian Mummy", "Adjanta Frescoes", and "Autumn Leaves" makes this abundantly clear, as it shows, too, that she had a standard of musical taste which went far beyond Hertel and Bayer, even if it did not reach so far into "modernity" as to include Stravinsky. Critics often called her old-fashioned because she danced

Hertel and Bayer but not Stravinsky. They overlooked the fact that most of her dancing was to
music which is neither as out-of-date as Hertel or
as "ultra-new" as Stravinsky. In music she remained between the devil and the deep blue sea.

Her own ballet, "Autumn Leaves", was musically satisfying in every way. Each phrase, each
nuance, each small *rubato* or *accellerando* of the
music was faithfully interpreted in the movements
of the dancers. My criticism of her as an erratic
interpreter of music absolutely does not apply to
this work, which was her very own. Here there
was no chopping up of musical phrases to suit the
dance, no liberties taken with tempo. The dance
and the music fitted like a piece of mosaic, because
Pavlova had taken infinite pains to study the music
and to evolve the exact gestures, movements and
groupings to interpret that music perfectly. Her
solo to the "D Flat Major Nocturne" in this ballet
was, as musical interpretation, the best dance in all
her repertoire.

Had she lived longer, there is no doubt that she
would have produced a ballet to the music of
Bach. After first hearing me play Bach's Toccata
and Fugue, she asked me to repeat them many

times, showing an increasing delight. Then we went together to hear, at a gramophone studio, the orchestral version of this work, which again Pavlova insisted on hearing several times. She then told me that her next new ballet would be to that music; but she died before carrying out her intention.

Perhaps I may fittingly append here this record of the last tribute I was able to pay to her memory. It is the programme of a concert which I conducted over the English radio at the request of our radio authorities, the British Broadcasting Corporation:

IN MEMORY OF

ANNA PAVLOVA

A Concert of the music to which she danced.

THE B.B.C. ORCHESTRA

Conducted by WALFORD HYDEN

Dionysius .... *Tscherepnine*
Pizzicato .... *Delibes*
Le Cygne (The Swan) .... *Saint-Saëns*
Valse Caprice .... *Rubinstein*
The Three Palms .... *Spendiarov*
Serenade .... *Drigo*

Pavlova

Variation (Coquetterie de Columbine)

Rimsky-Korsakov

Gavotte Pavlova (Glow Worm) .... *Lincke*

Bacchanale .... *Glazounov*

To be broadcast tonight at 9.35.

Among the ballets described in this chapter, I have not mentioned "La Bayadère", a ballet in which she had a tremendous success in Russia, but which she did not dance elsewhere. Neither have I described "La Peri", a ghostly and weird ballet of Paul Dukas, a difficult work in which the rhythm changes continually and the tempo is complicated to such an extent that Pavlova came to be sorry that she ever decided to dance it, though critics of the Diaghiliev school considered it one of her best achievements. There is also a pathetic little ballet "Les Trois Pantins de Bois", arranged by Pierre Chantel to the music of Michel Maurice Levy, in which she played, not very successfully, the part of a drooping young girl who perishes of cold and sickness. In her early days she also danced Glück's "Orpheus", which I cannot comment on here, not having seen it. I have also omitted a description of the very well-known "Coppelia", which was a favourite ballet of Adeline Genée in England before Pavlova came; and it should also be noted that in Russia Pavlova has danced "Esmeralda." She revived in her repertoire, towards the end of her life, her early ballet "The Awakening of Flora."

One of my greatest regrets is that I did not see her dance in "Spectre de la Rose" with Nijinsky as a partner. That wonderful youth was as great a dancer as Anna Pavlova — before his health broke down and suddenly he could remember nothing of all he had learned. His "elevation" was miraculous. Like Pavlova he had the ability to deceive the audience, so light-footed was he, and to convey the impression of not touching the floor at all. The pair together must have been superlatively entrancing, and probably the art of the Dance — whether ancient or modern — has never reached a higher moment than when Nijinsky and Pavlova were on the stage together, dancing to express the fragrance of a flower. Anna Pavlova never danced "Spectre de la Rose" afterwards.

CHAPTER X

Divertissements

THE public preferred watching short pieces
which they could understand to making the intellectual effort necessary to follow even the simplified
ballets which Pavlova presented. This is not surprising, if we realize that any great pianist, for example, has to make the same kind of concession to
his audience. As Rachmaninoff is better known by
his "Prelude" than by his greater works, so it was
with Pavlova and "The Swan." And just as the audience at a concert gives more applause to a short,
easily understandable item than to the intellecual
and emotionally sustained execution of a sonata, so
audiences were more enthused by Pavlova's divertissements than by even the greatest of her ballets.

She brought the divertissements to perfection
because she understood, as in "The Swan" and
many others, the importance of adding a dramatic
element to the dancing. Her divertissements were

quick character sketches, and they gave delight by this power of drama almost as much as by their excellence in dancing as such.

In the pieces described below, I include the better known of her dance numbers. The list makes no pretentions to completeness.

The Swan

It has been said that the idea for "The Swan" came while Anna Pavlova and Fokine were out walking in St. Petersburg. They saw some swans floating on a lake, and the idea was born that a dance to the motif of swans would be suitable for her. Subsequently Fokine arranged the dance for her to the music of Saint-Saëns, from "Les Fêtes des Animaux." The music of "Le Cygne" was particularly suitable for Pavlova's interpretation of the movements of the graceful white bird gliding upon the water's surface. To a 'cello solo, with harp accompaniment, suggesting the coolness of waters, she calmly and quietly floats at first, then with drooping pinions she begins the last fluttering movements which are stilled in quiet death.

"The Swan" is inseparably associated with Pavlova's name. It has been more copied by other dancers than any in her repertoire. The time came when she dared not omit it from a programme. She had danced it thousands of times, yet never with a relaxation of that wondrous mystic concentration and offering of herself to the symbolism. Clever people have come prepared to laugh at this so "hackneyed" dance — but have remained to pray. When, at her memorial performance in London in February, 1931, "Le Cygne" was played by the orchestra, the whole audience stood and many people said that they could see her faint white spirit on the stage.

Autumn Bacchanale

A *pas de deux* to the music of Glazounow's "Seasons", reconstructing more nearly the Dionysian spirit of the ancient Greek revels than any other art expression this generation is likely to witness. The abandon with which Pavlova threw back her head, seeming to yell with joy, as she whirled with her partner in a frenzy to the stamping 2/4 rhythm of the music, raised the pulse-beat of the whole audience to that primitive orgiastic rate which civilized decorum has banished from life. I have heard audiences yelling to her as though they too were dancing as she danced. One could almost hear the call "Io Pan! Euoi! Euoi!" and for a marvellous moment believe that the pagan gods had come to earth again.

Yet curiously enough, Anna Pavlova, in the opinion of the best critics, should never have danced this number. Her physique was, to say the least, unorthodox for a bacchante. She was too thin, too frail, to leap and bound like a plump mænad, cavorting in honour of Bacchus. Her genius was frailty. She was more suited for the expression of transient unreality than for Dionysian gusto. Perhaps it was for this reason that she abandoned the "Bacchanale" in her later years; yet so great was the versatility of her art that this is one of the dances by which she will be remembered.

Rondino

A little of nothing beautifully done to the music of Beethoven-Kreisler — a violin solo with string accompaniment. Her dress was a mauve floating crinoline and she carried a large white ostrich feather fan. "Rondino" is a woman's dance to captivate the male. Pavlova's lightness on the *point* was only intensified by the ballooning skirts and the waving fan with which she made play. At the last brisk chord of the music, she flicked the fan to cover herself completely from the audience and so remained, motionless. It was then that the audiences realised how much of the effect had depended upon her brilliant eyes; and with what artistry they had been entertained.

Gavotte Pavlova

A stately *pas de deux* in 4/4 time to the "Glow-Worm" music of Lincke. The costumes were of the Empire period, Pavlova in bonnet and a yellow silk dress with a train looped to her wrist; her partner in close-fitting velvet breeches and jacket, with lace cuffs and cravat. Here she was slender and elegant, beautiful of carriage, graceful in the manipulation of her train, a grand lady — and a coquette.

Les Papillons

To a 2/4 allegro movement from the music of Rimsky-Korsakov — a clarinet solo with string accompaniment — this gem of a dance lasted only forty seconds. It was a brilliant *pas de bourré* throughout, but it was her eyelashes and finger tips that one watched. Although the dance lasted for such a short time she was more exhausted by it than by any other in her repertoire, except the "Bacchanale." Every nerve in her body quivered as she danced — or as she hovered; not merely like a butterfly but a veritable butterfly dancing with the flowers in sunshine. So great a nervous effect was required that she could never remember the first two bars of the piece, which had to be hummed over to her before she began.

Valse Caprice

One of her earlier divertissements, a *pas de deux,* this valse, to the music of Rubinstein, was rarely included in the repertoire of Pavlova's later tours. It was a most energetic dance, expressing *joie de vivre* and girlish gaiety. Her pirouettes were amazing for their speed, a speed that has been described as dancing raised to the Pavlova-th power.

Romance

To Rubinstein's "La Nuit", she danced a *pas seul* which was like a Grecian elegy — graceful and calm, without passion, a beautiful dream in the night. Her costume was Grecian and perhaps of

PAVLOVA IN "THE BUTTERFLY"

all her dances this one showed best her control of flowing rhythm of the whole body, as contrasted with virtuosities of the toes or finger tips. "Romance", with its restful 4/4 time and its dreamy grace, generally followed something lively in the programme. Pavlova's showmanship!

The Dragon Fly

The music was Kreisler's "Schön Rosmarin", and the technique of the dance was similar to that used in "Les Papillons", but with more gesture and bodily movement and posture. If "The Swan" was her greatest *adagio,* the "Dragon Fly" was perhaps her finest allegro movement, in that it was sustained and dramatic — a counterpart in the light manner of what "The Swan" expressed with tragic power.

Pas Hongrois

Arranged by Novikoff, to the music of Glazounow, this divertissement was really a short ballet, in which twelve artistes of the Company took part. The music is from the ballet "Raymondo", arranged as a suite of dances for Pavlova and her Company. The costumes and dance were fantastically conceived in the Hungarian manner. The opening passage showed eight girls and four men dancing an *adagio* around Pavlova and her partner, in a dignified Hungarian style. Then follows a variation by a male dancer, and a big *coda* in which Pavlova had a lively solo. The finale (ensemble) was particularly enjoyed by the dancers themselves, so brilliant was the music. One of the best of her divertissements, the "Pas Hongrois" showed Russian ballet as it ought to be shown — precise, complicated and brilliant.

Californian Poppy

This divertissement — a striking choreographic conception — was one of the few in which an effect was achieved as much by costume and lighting as by the dancer's movements. It was a *pas seul* to the music of Tschaikowski — *moderato* 4/4 — and the image conveyed was the little drama of a poppy which opens during the day to the warmth of the sun and folds its petals in the evening when the sun's light has gone.

Her costume was of poppy red (the petals), her bodice green (the calyx), and on her head was a yellow wig (the stamen). First the flower opened one petal at a time and danced with joy in the sunshine; then at evening, as the light gradually faded, she drew one petal after another upwards to cover her face, with graceful shuddering movements until, at last, there was only enough light for the audience to see the poppy closed and asleep for the night. Pavlova often got the leader of the orchestra, during the interval, to play the music through to her before she danced it.

Syrian Dance

This was Pavlova's *other* dance to the music of Saint-Saëns; and it was as different from "The Swan" as it could possibly be. Here she was an Oriental courtesan, tempted by lecherous old merchants with gifts — and making fun of them. They bring her jewelry, mirrors in which to see her own beauty, and a richly shining piece of silk; all of which she accepts — and then runs away mockingly. The costumes, setting, and make-up and her voluptuous miming of Oriental passion and allure were perfect in their kind. She was a versatile woman, Pavlova.

Pavlova

Serenade

Music by Drigo. A classical harlequinade —
a *pas de deux*. I have already mentioned that Pavlova never gave this dance twice in the same way.
Her pirouettes varied in number each time and
her pose on the *point* lasted as long or as briefly
as she chose to make it last.

Coquetteries de Columbine

This is also a classical harlequinade, a *pas de trois,*
to Drigo's music. Pavlova, as a marquise, flirts with
two Pierrots — one melancholy, the other gay.
After she has excited them both, she trips away,
leaving them foolishly to embrace each other. In
her variation she maintained the *pas de bourré*
on the *point* for forty seconds. Here were fun,
coquetry and charm in abundance.

Christmas

Danced to one of Tschaikowski's best waltzes
("December") this number was a delicate little
ballet in eighteenth century costume. Pavlova, as
a young girl, is shown at the end of a Christmas
party, surrounded by admirers and loaded with

gifts, including a small Christmas tree. She dances with all the gallants but goes away with her true love, after most gracefully putting on a bonnet and a big cape, and bidding the others good-night.

Au Bal

A classical mazurka from Tschaikowski's grand ballet, "The Sleeping Beauty." Pavlova — in a long, fluffy blue dress, with long white gloves, a white wig with a small blue bonnet, and a dashing blue ostrich feather — is surrounded by six officers in the dress uniform of Hussars. She waves them away from her. They form a half-circle, sitting on chairs, while she dances the Polish Mazurka brilliantly, to their evident delight. This number was conceived and performed with éclat. The use of the chairs was unorthodox in ballet, but most effective.

La Gioconda

This was a little ballet — Poncinelli's "Dance of The Hours", with twelve girls entering as the clock strikes each hour — and Pavlova as the Spirit of Time. She danced here a notable *adagio*, show-

ing the abstract, relentless flow of Time, which
nothing can stop, which is ever smoothly moving.

The Lorelei

Another short ballet, to the music of Catalini.
Pavlova, as the Lorelei, dances with her Undines
and gnomes to enchant a young traveller. He falls
in love with the Lorelei, kisses her — and dies.
Whereupon she gloats soullessly and frisks away,
to the further planning of the destruction of mor-
tals. Quite an unusual theme for Pavlova, which
she danced with cruel realism.

The Champions

In writing this music for this *pas de trois,* I had
in mind, as did Romanov the choreographer, the
inclusion in Pavlova's repertoire of a twentieth-
century dance; and in theme at any rate it was the
only completely "modern" item in her repertoire.
She appeared as a tennis player, wearing a beret,
a white jumper and pleated skirt with short stock-
ings. The mime employed was that of a seventeen-
year-old schoolgirl, full of exuberance and vitality.
One of her partners was a golf champion, the other
a football captain. The gestures of the dance in-

PAVLOVA IN MEXICAN DANCE

cluded realistic rhythmic golf swings, the drib-
bling and passing of the football, and tennis vol-
leying and smashing *à la* Susanne Lenglen. She
also had a dance to another composition of mine,
"Polka Incroyable."

Mexican Dance

A favourite in her later repertoires, this dance,
to the music of Castilla Padilla, was first produced
in a bull ring during her Mexican tour. The excitable audience almost became delirious when they
saw Anna Pavlova dancing, on the point of her
toes, the Mexican steps usually danced on the heel.
A climax was when she danced around the brim
of a Mexican sombrero without touching the
crown. The crowd promptly threw their own best
hats into the ring for her to dance on!

As performed on a stage, the *décor* was richly
coloured, the warm yellow and red lighting and
scenery representing a huge Spanish shawl. The
costumes of the six dancers who took part were
real Mexican and boldly effective.

There was a short passage of mime following
her entrance. She appears in a petulant mood, as
the young girl discontented because she cannot

(239)

find a real interest in life. Suddenly she meets a young Mexican and life lights up. She whirls joyfully with him in a rapid, exciting dance, capable of enthusing even the dullest of onlookers.

Russian Dance

I conclude this survey of her divertissements with one of her favourites, one which she naïvely enjoyed whenever it was done — an expression of the fundamental Russian impulse to dance; a mystical, delicate and humourous racial impulse, without which, after all, the world would not have had its Pavlova.

The music is by Tschaikowski and Rubinstein. After a brilliant short overture, the curtain goes up to reveal eight girls in Russian peasant costume, dancing to a melancholy folk tune. A lad enters gaily and flirts with all the girls, dancing a merry and authentic Russian peasant dance. He mocks them, saying that his sweetheart will come soon, and that she is the best of all possible girls. Pavlova enters, dancing. She teases him and all the girls laugh at his discomfiture. Whereupon he produces a brilliant red kerchief and teases her in return. Pavlova snatches it from his hand and trium-

Pavlova

phantly dances with the flaming token. Her lad, reconciled, capers with joy, doing that difficult Russian step the "Presadka." In the finale, Pavlova runs away, followed by her lad doing the "Polzounok."

CHAPTER XI

"Plaudite, Amici"

WHEN I come now to write of the death of Anna Pavlova, it is with that feeling of numbed incredulity by means of which the mind avoids the worst things in life. The world without Pavlova is not the world we have known, who loved her. It is not merely that a woman, a friend, has died. It is that something marvellous has left the earth.

As the woman, the friend, she was a person unique, whose death would have been a great sorrow; but as Pavlova the Spirit of Dance, her death comes like a calamity. That her fragile, nervous, little body, so light as to seem unreal, should suffer real pain and die, that Pavlova has gone from us beyond recall, seems more than reason can accept.

Yet it is so. The most tragic words I have ever seen were the two words of a telegram sent from The Hague — "Pavlova morte." In common with hundreds of thousands of people on the earth, I was numbed with that news. I understand only too well the feeling that prompted a young Russian student in Paris actually to take his own life because the world without Pavlova was no longer worth living in. She had such a power over people.

To her faults as a woman, I, for one, was not blind, as the reader of this book knows; but what are her faults now? They do not matter. They will be forgotten so quickly that it would scarcely have been worth while to mention them, were it not that the whole truth is a more complete elegy than uncritical praise alone.

There cannot be another Pavlova. The world which produced her is changing, has changed; Pavlova's Russia unrecognizably so. As the rarest flower of a culture that has been doomed, she blossomed for a while, buffeted by the winds, like the last chrysanthemum of her own dance-poem "Autumn Leaves." But now a sudden gust has taken her from us and the petals are scattered.

Death came quickly. She died, when on tour with her Company, at The Hague, at twenty minutes past twelve in the morning of January 23, 1931. In December, she had completed a strenuous English tour during which, as I have already mentioned, she suffered agonies from an inflamed kneecap. A woman less fanatical in devotion to work would have taken a long rest cure before attempting, of all things, dancing as Pavlova danced. Instead, she allowed herself merely a few weeks' rest in the South of France, and planned another strenuous tour which was to begin in the New Year in Holland. After that she intended to travel quickly through Germany to Riga, and Reval; in perhaps a wistful nostalgia for her native land. Thence she was to have danced through Poland, Roumania, Serbia, Italy, and France before beginning yet another world tour.

But she never danced again after that evening in December in her beloved Hampstead. Travelling from the South of France on her way to Holland, she contracted a chill, after a railway accident which has already been described, in which the passengers had to turn out of the train and wait on the permanent way.

When she reached Paris she was ill, but refused to admit it. Her friends begged her to cancel the European tour and have a rest and medical treatment; but Pavlova would not listen to them. Rather than disappoint her public, rather than disband her Company, she decided to keep on dancing. She said, "I cannot allow myself to be ill. I must take myself in hand. I must work. I can stand any kind of physical pain. But if my nerves go, I am finished."

When she reached The Hague, acute pneumonia developed. Suddenly she seemed to collapse. It was as though there were no reserve of physical strength left to fight the disease, so much had she yielded up in a lifetime of dance. There was a chance of saving her by means of a trepanning operation on her ribs, which would have meant that she could never dance again. She refused to undergo the operation.

On the 22d of January, at six o'clock in the evening, the doctors pronounced her condition to be hopeless. Anna Pavlova was gasping for air. She said, "I am dying. Ease my pain." The doctors were unable to grant her request, and their injections gave no relief. At twelve midnight, she was delirious, and began asking for her Swan dress. Her voice became weaker. Suddenly she began moving her thin arms in the gestures of the dying swan. At twenty minutes past midnight her lungs failed and blood came from her throat. With a gasp, Anna Pavlova died. In death, there was a happy smile on her face.

All that day a crowd of people had been waiting outside the Hotel and telegrams were coming from every part of the world, anxiously asking about her state. The Queen of Holland sent messengers every three hours. It was a terrible moment when the doctors announced her end. Nobody could believe them.

Pianowski, her *maître de ballet,* arranged her limbs in the coffin. Her shroud was made by Manya, her wardrobe mistress for eighteen years. Her face in death was not shown to the members of her Company. They could not have borne to see her thus. She was brought to London, her home. The coffin was taken on board ship in a theatrical crate on which was painted "A. P."

The body was taken to the Russian Orthodox Church in Buckingham Palace Road. It was draped with the old Russian Imperial flag, which used to fly over the Czar's Consulate in London. While a Russian choir chanted, thousands of the Londoners who loved her filed through the Church and placed flowers on all that remained of Anna Pavlova. There were great wreaths mingled with little threepenny bunches of violets and lilies. At last, the coffin was not visible. Never were flowers a more appropriate farewell.

At the last, she was taken, mourned only by intimate friends, to the crematorium at Golders Green. Here the last sacred rites with Gregorian chants made solemn the quick change of her mortal body into ashes.

Of all that was strange in her death, there is nothing so affecting as the fact that with her last breath she called for her Swan dress. She died dancing and her epitaph might well be adapted from the words of the dying Beethoven — *"Plaudite amici, comoedia finita est."* Of her we might say "Applaud, friends, the dance is ended."

We who have seen her dying in the first act of "Giselle", to rise in the second act as a transfigured and immortally dancing spirit; we who have seen her stilled in the death of "The Swan" to arise gracefully as though brought back to life and uplifted on the gusts of public applause, will never see her dance any more.

What tangible relic of her genius is there to be handed down to future generations for the enlightenment and inspiration of mankind? The reader of this book who has seen Anna Pavlova dance will know what I mean when I speak of her incomparable swiftness of limb, of her histrionic intensity, of the subtle blend of perfected technique and expressionism in her dance. But to the reader of twenty years, fifty years, hence, there will be only photographs, showing a stilled instant of one who was the embodiment of movement. When all our generation is dead there will be nothing but these photographs and perhaps a few books like mine to keep alive her name, which itself is a melody.

This is a sad and bitter reflection for one who, throughout her world career, has been brought into contact with the inescapable fact of her genius. It is a sad and bitter reflection that a woman of genius concentrated emotionally in every fibre of her being and devoted to the expression of beauty in what is indisputably one of the arts, should pass at her death like a candle burned to the end, which can never give light again.

There have been other great dancers, such as Taglione, and before her Camargo, who have enthralled beholders in their day as Pavlova in ours. Yet now their names are but an echo of what they were. When Beethoven died, the Ninth Symphony could go on. Beethoven is always being played somewhere, and to his music there will never be an end, as long as music has any meaning. But the dancing of Anna Pavlova is ended now.

There will be other dancers, but not another Pavlova. We who have seen Pavlova dance have been in the presence of a mystery that cannot live again. This is the tragic bereavement which has numbed those who loved her. In her death as in her life she is a symbol of beauty's tragedy, the beauty that dies. Through her magic while she lived we came a little closer to an understanding of earth's secrets; and now that her so restless limbs are stilled at last, we are left wondering as at a vision that has passed and can never be reconstructed in our minds.

THE END

Index

EDWARD VII, KING, has Pavlova invited to England, 45

Egorova, Mme., *ballerina,* 74, 75

Egypt, visited by Pavlova, 65, 66, 96, 117, 118

"Egyptian Mummy, The," ballet, 15, 117, 142, 206–208, 211, 222

Eleusinian Mysteries, 5

Elizabeth, Empress, 22

"Esmeralda," ballet, 25, 35, 226

"Eunice," *pas de trois,* 31

FAIRBANKS, DOUGLAS, 125

"Fairy Doll, The," ballet, 15, 18, 123, 164, 186, 190–192, 216, 221

Fazer, M., manager, 32

"Fille Mal Gardée, La," ballet, 15, 49–51, 76, 164, 186, 189, 190, 221

Finck, Hermann, waltz by, 72

"Firebird," 185

Flitch, J. E. Crawford, *Modern Dancing and Dancers,* 23

Fokine, musical director, 129, 187; takes part in organizing strike among members of the Imperial Ballet, 29; impressed by opinions of Isadora Duncan, 30, 31; and "The Swan," 228

"GAVOTTE PAVLOVA," divertissement, 13, 164, 177, 178, 204, 231

Genée, Adeline, dancer, 47, 48, 226

Gerdt, instructor of Pavlova, 25, 28

Germany, visited by Pavlova, 59, 60, 66, 95, 96; orchestra considered a military organization in some parts of, 138. *See also* Berlin

"Gioconda, La," divertissement, 237, 238

"Giselle," ballet, 14, 15, 25, 40, 59, 60, 62, 164, 186, 211, 217–219, 247

Glasgow, 173

Glazounow, Alexander K., 84, 221, 222, 229, 233

Grahn, Lucille, dancer, 47

Grimaldi, Giovanni Francesco, dancer, 35

Grisi, Carlotta, dancer, 47

HAVANA, visited by Pavlova, 61

Helsingfors, Pavlova at, 32

Holland, visited by Pavlova, 66, 95

Home for Russian Children in Paris, Pavlova's private charity, 101

Hyden, Walford, programme

Pavlova, Anna, *(Continued)*
birds and flowers, 69, 70, 126,
127; *corps-de-ballet,* 73, 74;
anecdotes of, 75, 109–111,
113–115; her practising, 77;
her outlook on life, 79; her
charm, 79; her fondness for
sculpture, 80; her modeling,
81; her dress, 81–83; her
diet, 83; visited by her
mother, 86, 87; her Russian
habits, 87–89; receives illuminated scroll signed by
members of Moscow Art
Theatre, 88; her Ballet Company on tour, 90–127;
itinerary of English provincial tour of 1927, 94, 95; a
specimen year of her life of
touring, 95, 96; in Java, 97–
99; her interest in daily lives
of people, 99, 100; her way
with children, 100, 101; her
private charity (Home for
Russian Children in Paris),
101; her care for the members of her Company, 101–
105; imposed upon by beg-
ging-letter writers, 103–105;
salaries paid by, 105–108;
her ruthlessness, 108, 109;
her sense of fun, 112, 113;
her introspective mysticism,

117; had little interest in
reading, 119; her interest in
painting, 119, 120; her stubborn determination, 122; her
interest in cinematography,
123–126; her addiction to
work, 128–151, 161–166; her
apparent crassness in the interpretation of music, 141–
143; regarded herself as infallible, 143, 144; her learning of a new dance, 144–
147; the photographing of,
147; her "auditions," 148–
150, 165; as a dancer, 152–
170; was an independent
thinker in the dance, 156–
158; loved applause, 159; led
a physically austere life, 161;
a typical programme of, 162–
165; the amount of travelling
done by, 169, 170; mishaps
to, 171–181; her selection of
ballets, 182, 186, 221–224;
why she left Diaghiliev, 185;
revised her ballets, 186, 187;
her repertoire of ballets, 188–
219, 225, 226; her Oriental
dancing, 203, 204; never
subordinated herself to the
music, 220; programme of
concert broadcasted in memory of, 224, 225; her diver-